In the Twilight with God

In the Twilight with God

A Critique of Religion in the Light of Man's Glassy Essence

BENJAMIN W. FARLEY
foreword by DONALD McKIM

CASCADE *Books* • Eugene, Oregon

IN THE TWILIGHT WITH GOD
A Critique of Religion in the Light of Man's Glassy Essence

Copyright © 2014 Benjamin W. Farley. All rights reserved. Except for brief quotations in critical publications or reviews, no part of this book may be reproduced in any manner without prior written permission from the publisher. Write: Permissions, Wipf and Stock Publishers, 199 W. 8th Ave., Suite 3, Eugene, OR 97401.

Cascade Books
An Imprint of Wipf and Stock Publishers
199 W. 8th Ave., Suite 3
Eugene, OR 97401

www.wipfandstock.com

ISBN 13: 978-1-62564-631-6

Cataloging-in-Publication data:

Farley, Benjamin Wirt, 1935–.

    In the twilight with God : a critique of religion in the light of man's glassy essence / Benjamin W. Farley, with a foreword by Donald K. McKim.

    xvi + 122 p.; 23 cm—Includes bibliographical references and index.

    ISBN 13: 978-1-62564-631-6

    1. God—History of doctrines. 2. God—Comparative studies. 3. Religion—Philosophy. 4. Religion and science. I. McKim, Donald K. II. Title.

BT98 F37 2014

Manufactured in the USA.

Unless otherwise noted, Scripture quotations are from the New Revised Standard Version Bible, Copyright 1989, Division of Christian Education of the National Council of the Churches of Christ in the United States of America; reprinted with permission. All rights reserved.

Dedicated to the memory of
George Lawrence Abernethy
James Slicer Purcell, Jr.
and
Lewis Bevens Schenck
Professors respectively of Philosophy, Literature,
and Religion, Davidson College, 1950s:
Ne Plus Ultra

Table of Contents

Foreword by Donald K. McKim ix

Introduction xiii

1 The Inescapable Question 1
2 That Than Which None Greater Can be Conceived 9
3 The Ground of Being 21
4 Language, Truth, and Metaphor 29
5 A Critique of the Philosophical Arguments for the Existence of God 38
6 Science and the Universe 44
7 The Voice of Being Speaks Many Languages 51
8 Beyond Good and Evil 60
9 The Ballast of Skepticism 69
10 The Dynamics of Doubt and Its Anodyne Faith 81
11 Redemption and Redeemers 88
12 The Light that Enlightens Everyone 93
13 The Hiddenness of God 101
14 *Magna Est Veritas*: A Postscript 107

Appendix A: Athens and Jerusalem 111

Appendix B: Karl Barth's Rejection of the *Analogia Entis* 115

Bibliography 119

Foreword

How then do we think of God?
This question has been part of human experience for millennia. The history of the human race has, in various expressions, dealt with this question. It is inborn, innate—in what ways do we conceive of a "God" who is beyond us? What, or who, is the power, the presence, the reality that we perceive? Our perceptions are not on the sensory level. They are deeper. They are intellectual; but more. They point us to an actuality, a veracity—a truth—that defies all attempts to give an exhaustive definition. Our perceptions, in unformed and inexplicable ways, nudge us to a sense of authentic truth that we cannot capture within ourselves. But that reality is there. It transcends us, goes beyond who we are as individuals, as the human race. Yet it is real. It is clothed in mystery and unknowing. But we cannot deny there is something "beyond." Our thinking, contemplations, and deep reflections open us to the possibilities that our human consciousness is not the only reality that exists. There is more. There is—shall we say it?—God.

This quest for a "God reality" has occupied human thinking through the ages. It has taken many forms. Some are rigorously intellectual. Some are introspective and contemplative. Others are pragmatically oriented: "It can't hurt to believe in 'God,' can it? Maybe it can help my daily life." Philosophers, theologians, and "ordinary people" in their own ways try to come to grips with a "God reality." Our personalities, orientations, and proclivities can draw us to one kind of approach or another. What "makes sense" to one person, may not be so compelling to someone else.

But we think, we explore, we listen to any input that can help us make sense of who we are; and who "God" might be. There are many options to explore, many paths to follow. In the ages past, others have wrestled with our questions. So the better part of wisdom is to listen to what our fellow-humans have had to say. As we survey the wide range of opinions and approaches, we may find something that makes sense. The "penny may drop" for us—we may come to new insights that can affect us. Our whole life orientation can be changed if we recognize a "God reality" that has to this point remained hidden from us. One never knows where following a path may lead!

This book by Benjamin Farley will help all such seekers and questers. It will help all those who want to open their minds to the wisdom of the past. This book enables us to listen to what some of the best human minds have had to say about "God" and what this "God" may be like.

So the pages ahead are a treasure for all who want to engage the God question. Here, Farley shows himself a masterful interpreter of main approaches to the issue of God as probed by philosophers and theologians. They have given their best thought to this issue. Now Farley leads us through their teachings, arguments, and musings. He is a splendid teacher in laying out what the great thinkers have thought. To investigate the thought of those who have devoted such sustained thinking to this issue is work worth doing. These chapters unlock the rich resources that can help us—whomever we are—to contemplate answers to the question: "How then do we think of God?"

The questions relating to "What is God?" or "Who is God?" are many. Farley explores these here, too. He considers issues of language and truth, science and the universe, God and evil, redemption and redeemers, the hiddenness of God, and others. These come at the "God question" in light of the realities we encounter in life. A "God" who is removed from the lives of humans can be an intellectual construct. But is there more?

There is the "God of the philosophers" and also the "God of faith." Philosophy uses the best of our human intellectual thinking to reason and argue and postulate ideas—even the idea of God. "Religion" stands in a complementary position to philosophy at this point. Religion—which is constituted by "faith" in some form, looks to what may be true beyond the limits of our intellects, reason, and postulates. It looks to what it perceives as "revelation," how the reality of God is made known to humans in ways we ourselves cannot construct. In the religion of Christianity, for example, God's revelation is considered to be conveyed through the Scriptures of the Old and New Testament. In Christianity, God's revelation of God's own self is believed to be in the person of Jesus of Nazareth, who is "the true light, which enlightens everyone" (John 1:9). So in our "quest for God," religion can speak to the deep needs of the human heart, convey a reality that our minds alone cannot discover. As the philosopher Blaise Pascal (1623–62) put it: "The heart has its reasons, which reason does not know."

So we must be open to religion as well as philosophy in our seeking after "God," or in our recognition of a God who has come to us as humans. Faith and reason can complement each other. In the Christian tradition, St. Augustine (354–430) used the motto: "Faith seeking understanding." Faith is supplemented by reason to understand more fully what faith means. Reason helps us explore the realities of the world, the human self—and God.

The book before us helps us understand philosophy and theology, reason and faith. The author is a sure guide in all these dimensions. As he writes, "The role of reason exercises a central place in the study, while mankind's 'spiritual' and 'mystical' quest is equally dignified." This pays attention to the realities in which we live. We are people of reason; we are also spiritual people. Humans are "fearfully and wonderfully made" as the Old Testament psalmist put it (Ps 139:14). The complexities of human life sort themselves out in one way or another in different people. But paying attention to philosophy *and* theology; to faith *and* reason is surely what brings fullness to our lives—to the life of the mind and the life of the spirit.

This book will open new ways of understanding and of faith. Learn here from an experienced guide who unlocks the insights of some of the world's greatest thinkers. Read appreciatively, be challenged and stimulated, and ponder anew the great question: "How then do we think of God?

Donald K. McKim
Germantown, Tennessee

Introduction

CRITIQUES OF RELIGION ARE as ancient as mankind. Not even the gods of the Gilgamesh Epic are spared criticism. It was only after the good citizens of Uruk complained about Gilgamesh's behavior that the gods created a lover, Shamhat, and later a companion, Enkidu, to distract the mighty hero from his carefree exploits. In time, a mortal flood of mankind's woes would flow from Gilgamesh's adventures, along with his excitement and passion, prowess and loss that came to be viewed as a universal window onto humankind's existence.

Plato, Aristotle, Epicurus, Cicero, and Epictetus added their voices, too. Their goal was to clarify as well as question the role of the gods in society, or analyze the essence of religion in their respective city-states or, in Cicero and Epictetus' case, the Roman Republic and later Empire. Certainly, for the above, the emerging tendency among philosophers was to emphasize reason over ritual, and essence over the individual, while still endorsing personal belief in the gods for political and/or idealistic and mystical purposes. One has to wait for the modern era of British Empiricism, of Locke, Berkeley, and Hume, or for Voltaire in France, or Kant in Prussia before a genuine critique of religion settles in; although Cicero's *De Natura Deorum Academica* was an authentic, critical essay on the gods as believed in by the Epicurean, Stoic, and Academic schools of his time.

The critique offered in the following study is both critical of religion and a defense of religion. It follows a critical methodology insofar as it examines religious developments and/or depictions of the divine in conceptual forms that a scientific understanding of the universe cannot support. On the other hand, it proffers criteria by means of which belief in the existence of God and an understanding of God's "Being" may best be measured from a philosophical and religious perspective.

The study incorporates both historical and thematic approaches, as well as exploring phenomenological and metaphysical interests. It seeks to be positive toward religion wherever the latter proves to be a reasonable answer to humankind's search for meaning and value. In that respect, a human being's spiritual needs are considered an inseparable aspect of his/her existentiality. God is not maligned as a "delusion," yet any embracement of the divine or of life's highest order is expected to live up to universal and beneficial dimensions that edify rather than demean the human condition. To that extent, the role of reason exercises a central place in the study, while mankind's "spiritual" and "mystical" quest is equally dignified. In the author's mind, any attempt to delineate the boundaries of a critique of religion that excludes either would not qualify as a genuine critique of the subject.

In particular, the book's interest lies in exploring definitions of God that speak to the heart as well as to the mind, to the theological academy as well as to the disciplines of philosophy and science. In an ideal world both science and religion, anthropology and religious studies would be on the same page, facets of a unified holistic view that elevate mankind to its highest level. That is not the case today but remains a worthy aim. Certainly, the human spirit is large enough, not merely to consider, but to accommodate and find satisfaction in both views.

As for my use of the word "existential," I mean all that defines one in his or her individual self-understanding. It includes *cognitive* as well as *ontological* and *phenomenological* factors; in addition, *therapeutic* and *aesthetic* nuances. As *cognitive*, religion, if it is to be effective, must speak to our self-understanding with honesty as well as acknowledge the reality of the world as science perceives it. Inasmuch as that occurs, it should be capable of addressing our genuine, unashamed questions about life, our destiny, and the universe. As *ontological*, it should enable us to confront reality as it is, the world in all its concurrences and eons of evolution and development, while embracing our individuality in all our joy and angst, excitement and dread, as self-determined and self-determining beings. As *existential*, religion should provide us with a therapeutic uplift regarding our place in the universe. It should not leave us feeling morose or helpless. It should speak to the core of our selfhood, grip us with urgency and relevance, not as we might wish our lives were, but as they actually are, if they are to be transformed. As such, it should encourage us to assume responsibility for

INTRODUCTION

our own life, face with rigor whatever alienation and remorse we have experienced or for which we are culpable. Finally, as a pleasant codicil, it should open our eyes to the realm of *aesthetics*, to the beauty and wonder of the universe, to the splendor and majestic glory of every galaxy, crystalline star, down to the fragile existence of every sentient being.

Benjamin W. Farley
Columbia, SC

CHAPTER 1

The Inescapable Question

THE QUESTION IS INFINITELY more than "does God exist?" or even, "does it matter that God exists?" Either question is multi-faceted and incorporates a sequel of related questions within itself. Why? Because words like "God" and "exists" are functions of the definitions we assign them. To assume that either implies an independent existence beyond language is part of the problem we cannot escape. Indeed, complicating and inseparable from the preceding statement is the age-old distinction between objectivity and subjectivity. How do we ever get out of our subjectivity to know anything objective? We shall examine this in chapter 4. Still, the dilemma persists. Does God exist objectively, independent of a human self, or is God purely a function of our subjective encounter with the self as we relate to the world?

Does that mean that we can never attain a definitive answer to either question? Most contemporaries would maintain that no one knows the truth about God in any scientific sense; only faith can make that leap. This side of faith, ambivalence will always prevail. Nonetheless, there are sound philosophical and religious considerations that have sustained mankind in their leaps of faith. We shall seek to examine these as the critique unfolds.

By this I do not mean to sound that I know something that nobody else knows. God hasn't singled me out or endowed me with a privileged position. Across the centuries, however, religious persons have experienced a Self within the self of their self-consciousness that engages them in dialogue, if not an encounter with a deeper Self whose presence is totally unmediated. One thinks of biblical Abraham and the ease with which

YHWH converses with him and he with YHWH, or the sudden appearance of Krishna in the chariot with the young Arjuna who is on his way to battle in that epic story of the *Bhagavad Gita*. For years, Western theologians have addressed this phenomenon under the heading of "transcendence," even identifying the self's awareness of that Other as the self's "encounter" with God. In today's culture, however, such encounters with any mystical Self, especially defined as God, are politely, if not openly, rejected. On the contrary, it is argued that any Self within the self is nothing more than the mind's capacity to address itself, or one's inner self simply speaking to the self. Even more likely, it is a "meme," a gene, in accordance with Richard Dawkins' theory, by means of which mankind has been able to cope with life and survive over the eons of evolution. In fact, during the nineteenth century, the philosopher Ludwig Feuerbach argued that mankind's "innate" sense of God was little more than an objectification of one's inner-self, purified and projected onto the screen of infinity as God. Today's world is simply more comfortable with assessing any awareness of "divine presence" as an aspect of one's biological self, influenced by cultural preference, rather than an awareness of an Eternal Order that stands outside the self.

Taking issue with all this, however, is the late existentialist Jewish philosopher Martin Buber. With passion he argued that God is not a condition that exists merely within human beings, or a transcendent principle whose existence is dependent upon the mind of man. Rather, God is truly independent and exists over against man, yet constantly in dialogue with man. More must be said of this later, but suffice it to state that the majority of present-day empirical-minded people find themselves more under the influence of skeptics of religion than believers in the reality of God as one who exists outside human subjectivity.

Had one been born in the East, it is likely that one's sense of the mystical self would be identified with the Buddha essence, or, at least in Hinduism, with one of Vishnu's descents, or as that Name not even the Taoists dare name. The phenomenon of "transcendence" has been known for centuries. Yet, for all the wisdom attached to the major religions and their prophets, priests, and mystics, we still do not know *with certainty* the truth about God, or for that matter the truth about ourselves vis-à-vis the phenomenon of transcendence.

Both Plato and Descartes longed for certainty. So also did St. Augustine. All three labored to discover the absolute grounds on which one might establish a foundation for what can be known about anything. For Plato, it was the realm of eternal ideas, or universals which the mind grasps, that became his foundation for knowing what is good, true, and real; for Descartes, it was the self-evident truths that his doubting mind could not deny that became "indubitable" for him; for Augustine, it was the illuminating power of faith that enabled him to understand the created universe, thus allowing his restive heart to find rest in God.

Each in his way established a level of certainty to which he could entrust his life. But their world of transcendent certitude is no longer believable for many today. This is especially the case in the light of contemporary science's knowledge of the universe and of human evolution. In the mind of skeptical science, belief in God is more of a detriment than a blessing, more of a step back into ignorance than an advancement toward enlightenment. Thus, religious persons are compelled to explore anew the truth about themselves and God. No one can ever possess with innocence Plato, Augustine, or Descartes' certitude again, but one can examine the phenomenon of the sense of the presence of God, along with mankind's philosophical and religious arguments for God, insofar as any of the above can be objectively studied and critiqued. Moreover, it is a task that can be relished, as much as Sisyphus relished his, who from morning to evening rolled the stone of his existence up the dark hill of destiny, even though his stone rolled back down in the smudge of a purple dusk. In the same way that Samson placed his hands against the pillars of the Philistines' temple to bring down its stones about their pagan heads, so too contemporary humankind can apply the synapses of reason against today's pillars of objection to recover what can be postulated about God.

What are some of the pillars that must come down? A partial list might include the following:

Exclusivity. As difficult as this may be for established religions, especially Protestantism, Catholicism, and the Reformed Tradition, or facets of Judaism, Islam, and Buddhism, few, if any, global-minded persons today would maintain that their religion alone enjoys an inviolable, *privileged position* among the competing views of God. Such confidence may have served cultural purposes and political aspirations up through the late nineteenth century, but the self-advancement of one religion over others can neither be proven to be true nor fruitful for international dialogue. A militant Christianity, zealot Zionist movement, or resurgent Islam may enjoy support among respective constituents, but they fail to address the global sighs for peace and wellbeing that demand redress in our time. To bind

God to a single religion, as if God's voice cannot be heard in the universal hunger and hope, insight and comfort of other faiths, or their theological views, eviscerates any unconditional goodness that the subject could hope to offer. All deserve to be explored as windows onto the Eternal, until their darker shadows obscure the view.

The assumption that one's religion *actually speaks unequivocally for God* is a second pillar that requires Samson's nudge. In truth, no one can claim that his or her religion speaks solely for God while others do not. At best, each represents a culture's collected thoughts, or inherited traditions, or personal convictions of divine encounters, echoing one's deep and abiding personal longings. The Ineffable, of its very necessity, would have to transcend anything mankind has thought about the divine or attributed to God. Thus, Isaiah could imagine God descrying: "For your ways are not my ways, nor your thoughts my thoughts" (Isa 55:8). His bold assertion still stands as one of mankind's greatest insights. No one today can claim to speak unequivocally for God. Such "speaking" testifies primarily to the speaker's heritage, background, or cultural milieu. At best, one can strive to appreciate the religious experiences of others, or, whenever possible, demonstrate respect for the varied hierophanies that manifest the Holy.

Revelation. Revelation has often been defined as that moment of moments in the light of which all other moments become intelligible. H. Richard Niebuhr advanced this view with powerful persuasion. Yet, as convincing as this insight sounds, each religion savors its own revelatory moment or moments, challenging any hope of discovering a universal moment or hierophany that illuminates all humankind's other moments. That means that "revelations" are also bound by time and culture, language and the historical exigencies of locale and era. To argue that one's "revelation" is superior to another's is a facet of cultural-centricity, which requires an authentic and humble willingness to test the Spirit of grace and insight it has to offer.

Related to revelation is each religion's dogma concerning *authoritative sources*. These consist of sacred writings, viewed as divinely inspired and often considered inerrant and infallible in order to establish a religion's unassailable veracity. Whether it is the Holy Bible, the Quran, the *Bhagavad Gita*, the *Dhammapada*, or *Tao Te Ching*, each collection claims to be a depository of sacred wisdom, if not the actual words of God or its founder, thus making that religion's scriptures inviolable. Rather than each being the sole source of God's will or of God's self-revelation, each requires investigation and scrutiny of its own. None can be taken on face value without passing the bar of what we know to be true, just, and in sync with the universe.

Literalism also constitutes a formidable obstacle. The belief that God created the universe in six days, or that Moses literally parted the waters of the Red Sea, or that dead bodies and/or deceased souls can be resurrected to an eternal life, or that we are reincarnations of preexisting souls, or that multiple Buddha-lands await the Buddha's faithful followers, or that each Dalai Lama is an actual reincarnation of his predecessor's spirit, or that the Shiite Mahdi or Christian Messiah may return at some future time, clashes with contemporary humankind's knowledge about anything we cherish as true. It stands in stark opposition to the Enlightenment and what we know about the universe, its age, origin, natural laws, and evolving geo-physical concurrences. Literalism has done much to thwart the truth about the universe in which we live. In some instances it has led to a plethora of fundamentalist beliefs that do more to divide the world than foster common hope. At other times it has promoted an intellectual and spiritual darkness that belies the very truth it portends to herald. Christianity, Islam, Judaism, along with barbaric Hindu groups, share equal blame for fostering fundamentalist groups that insist that God supports their radical views, thereby justifying their acts of violence, abuse, and terrorism. Such views have created fanatical dreams of creating fascist theocracies opposed to every idea of freedom and liberty that the last four centuries of social contract democracies have sought to establish.

Superstition. Even Jesus opposed superstition, denying the belief that parental sin was the causal factor of a young man's blindness (John 9:3). As an exorcist and Palestinian sage, he labored within the framework of his culture's medical and therapeutic limits to heal people. He discouraged the "healed" from making unsubstantiated claims, encouraging them rather to submit to the religious practices of the time, or just remain silent. He was not after fame for himself. It was thrust upon him by the discouraged, downcast, and disenfranchised populace of the time. Only later was their movement championed by a more educated and disenchanted generation of leaders whose unhappiness with the politico-religious policies of the Roman Empire compelled them to look elsewhere. The latter represent that long line of dedicated bishops and priests who transformed the Jesus Movement into a powerful Western religion by the time of Charlemagne.

Miracles. The philosopher David Hume argued that miracles are the weakest line of evidence on which to build truth. Reason, experience, and observation coalesced for him to provide mankind's surest "ultimate standard." He defined a miracle as "a violation of the laws of nature," which experience cannot verify.[1] Nor has any sufficient number of "unquestioned [men] of good sense, education and learning" by their observations and witness ever secured confidence in favor of miracles. He offered as a maxim the principle that "objects of which we have no experience resemble those of which we have." Only the uninformed, awed by "surprise and wonder," are led astray to embrace the miraculous.

This isn't to say that sacred writings aren't filled with "wonder and surprise," or even saga, legend, poetry, and mystical visions. Certainly, Paul Tillich's definition of "miracle" supersedes Hume's altogether and is far more profound (see chapter 3). Thanks to Tillich, stories of wonder and surprise fall under appropriate categories of interpretation and need not be viewed as literal observable experiences, or as Hume's "violations of the laws of nature." Granted that God exists, astute and penetrating minds would still constitute God's greatest gift to humanity. In that regard, gullibility is not a virtue, nor has it ever been. True, Martin Luther castigated "reason," referring to it as a "cunning, rascally power" and frequently denounced its followers. But his critique was aimed principally against the schoolmen of the mid-to-late medieval period, and "those who follow the light of reason and go no farther than they consider right, godly, and good." The latter he deemed no better than "horses and asses."[2] His harsh words, however, were intended to bolster faith in God and God's salvation rather than in human pride and self-righteousness. To that extent, the limits of reason in its ascent to God are well taken.

Exclusivity, privileged position, revelation, authoritative sources, literalism, superstition, and a fascination with miracles constitute unfortunate barriers that do more to cloud an understanding of God than to illuminate the subject.

If the truth about God, or God himself, is knowable, one would think it would have to address the following criteria:

Unity or Divine Oneness. One cannot imagine that God would be subject to, or limited by, different perspectives. Zen, Taoism, and the Theravada

---

1. See Hume, *An Inquiry Concerning Human Understanding*, Sec. X, quoted in John Hick (ed.), *Classic and Contemporary Readings*, 110.
2. Luther, *Luther's Works*, vol. 14, 201, 15.

School of Buddhism view the divine as impersonal, if not non-existent at all. Their focus is on a way of life that conforms to the flow of the universe, not on a way of life lived in praise and dependence on a transcendent deity. God as God would transcend both personal and non-personal definitions and lead to the principle below.

Trans-global. God would be the God of all people, of all races, in all places, in all regions, in all cultures, across all time. Our perceptions of God might be limited, but the God behind them would be the same. Whether God is called the Buddha essence, Shiva, Brahma, Vishnu, Allah, the Holy Trinity, or El-Shaddai, God would still be God. However God is named, it is the same God, the highest truth about the universe, that is named. The notion that Allah, Vishnu, or any other name refers to a false god would have to be rejected. God is God, one and the same, anywhere and everywhere. The names are of human invention, even YHWH's—as soul wrenching as that very idea might be for the Judeo-Christian faiths.

Reflected in the Universe. This brings us back to Hume, if not long before Hume. The writer of the Wisdom of Solomon captured it best: "For from the greatness and beauty of created things comes a corresponding perception of their Creator" (Wis 13:5). That is why a god who abrogates the intricacies of his or her own created order becomes suspect. The authors of the book of Genesis wisely open with God pronouncing the "expanding" universe as "good." Any religion or perception of God that fails to do justice to the existent universe *as it is* automatically raises suspicion. This is especially the case with fundamentalist groups that deny evolution—a reality whose truth has been demonstrated again and again by the world's leading paleontologists, anthropologists, and biologists. Even Dawkins' theory about "memes" deserves consideration, as undoubtedly our DNA has been programmed to carry and replicate units of cultural, social, and survivable-skills in our physiological database. Similarly, those who balk at the Big Bang theory do so in complete misunderstanding of what astrophysicists have been able to establish. The universe is a stunning, unfolding, expanding phenomenon for all to witness and study, at times bizarre and filled with beauty, at times maverick and shimmering with gases of dying and exploding stars; nonetheless a wonder that has been in existence for billions of years. Hardly a dreary and empty world, separated by light years of vacuous spaces, the universe awaits our continuing discoveries of its galactic and brilliant grandeur.

Beyond Good and Evil. Our definitions of good and evil do not apply directly with reference to God. Good and evil are functions of our human journey, dependent on experiences and language that stretch back to the dawn of time. Since the ascendance of Homo sapiens, good and bad, just and unjust, permissible and taboo have enjoyed a long history of debate and development. Such definitions must be held in reserve when applied to God. We cannot fathom the mind of God, let alone God's intentions this side of eternity. What God favors, or disfavors, remains out of reach to the keenest of God's discerning servants and wisely requires reflection and criticism. One can only posit suppositions based on reason and revelatory moments of insight that are attune to the human experience. Moreover entropy, death, and decay are as endemic to life as life itself. Both witness to the nature of the universe and, therefore, to the mystery of its creation or origin. Hinduism's notion of Shiva, the destroyer, who dances within his ring of fire, may be closer to the truth about the creative power of God than static Western concepts of an unchanged and unchanging Being. Even the biblical story of Genesis pictures divine creation in dynamic terms, hardly static or unchanging. In the same way, Hinduism's devotion to Vishnu, the god who sustains and enlightens all souls, equally celebrates the creative and propagating mystery of both stars and mankind alike. Even Christianity has its Lucifer, though it has separated him from the being of God, yet not from God's court.

Beyond objectivity and subjectivity. In many respects this is the Catch-22. To confine God to either domain defeats the whole quest to know God. God cannot be *a physical thing* per se, bound by the limitations that pertain to *physical objects* (i.e., contained within space and time), culminating in self-fulfillment only to perish. God as God would have to be more, or, if possessing *being*, be envisioned as the dynamic, creative, magnificent reality behind the electro-magnetic intricacies of the universe. Nor can God be confined to the domain of immanence alone. For again, God would be bound by the totality of finite entities as a function of their subjectivity; a prisoner within the phenomenon of each contingency's sentience or sheer, physical beingness. Transcendent yet immanent, necessary yet engaged in the contingent, God encounters humans as the mystery in, of, and behind their very being.

The above represent but a few principles to be considered. They are criteria that I have come to believe are very important. One might regard them as normative principles that guide what follows in this study. At this juncture, however, a more specific examination of Western Christianity's concept of God deserves review.

CHAPTER 2

That Than Which None Greater Can be Conceived

WE OWE THE ABOVE phrase to Anselm. It ranks among mankind's sterling efforts to define God in the most fitting way. If God exists, God would have to be that than which none greater can be conceived. Therefore it must follow that God exists, for if God did not, then God would not be that than which none greater can be conceived. For, as Anselm reasoned, that which exists in actuality and not in thought only is greater than that which exists in thought only. Thus, God must exist, if God is that than which none greater can be conceived.[1]

Anselm explained that he was not trying to prove God's existence on the basis of reason alone. Rather, he described his position as one of "faith seeking understanding." Hence, based on the mind's ability to think with logical clarity, he was able to posit an argument couched in unassailable analytical form. In fact, by Anselm's very definition, it is impossible for God not to exist, or God would not be "he" whom none greater can be thought. All of this hinges, of course, on Anselm's supposition that irrefutable statements imply the truth of their content, as Paul Tillich surmised in his own writings. Such statements possess existential import. They point to a reality that truly exists. His position today is known as the ontological argument. Of course, Anselm was building on a system of truth that owed its origin to a long line of predecessors, among whom were the Semites, Plato, Aristotle,

---

1. See Anselm's *Proslogion*, *The Mayor Works*, 83–87.

and later philosophers such as Philo of Alexandria, Plotinus, and Pseudo-Dionysius's works, namely: *Divine Names* and *Celestial Hierarchy*.

Though gone from the present scene, few have phrased the question of God better than Alfred North Whitehead in his book *Religion in the Making*, first published in 1926. Therein Whitehead voiced his question much as we have: "What do you mean by 'God'?"[2] He labeled it the "fundamental religious dogma," from which all others are subsidiary. Drawing on the wealth of Western philosophical thought, he offered the Semite definition of God as: "a definite personal individual entity, whose existence is the one ultimate metaphysical fact, absolute and underivative, who decreed and ordered the derivative existence [of] the actual world."[3] This view he called "the extreme doctrine of transcendence." But for all its appeal, he noted it comes burdened with two principal difficulties. First, it places God outside all "metaphysical rationalization." And second, it evades any proof. The only rational one, Whitehead concluded, was Anselm's ontological argument, or René Descartes' later modification of the same. Descartes extended Anselm's proof by defining God as "a supremely perfect Being." As such, existence would have to be one of God's attributes, or else God would fail to be the "supremely perfect Being."

It is Plato to whom Anselm, Augustine, and so many other Western thinkers owe their doctrine of "extreme transcendence." In truth, Plato's "God" is a symbol of the highest Good a mind can know as it contemplates the noblest of enduring ideas to which the mind can ascend. In his dialogue *Timaeus*, Plato's interlocutor asks: "What is that which always is and has no becoming?" Of course, the answer is God. For things that are in a state of becoming and later perish cannot be said to be "real," that is, to possess a "complete" state of existence, since they are in a perpetual state of transformation. Moreover, physical things in particular are little more than derivatives of our opinions of sense perception. And since they are visible, tangible, and impermanent, they cannot have existed always. Therefore, to exist at all, they must have had a beginning or a creator. This creator would have to be eternal and without beginning himself. Timaeus, the interlocutor, concludes that this has to be "God," who always has been and enjoys "complete existence" with no "becoming." In addition, since life is good at many levels, God must also be good, who as the greatest good desired

---

2. Whitehead, *Religion in the Making*. 66.
3. Ibid.

that "all things should be as [much] like himself as they could."[4] Thus, as the dialogue posits, out of the visible sphere of restless matter, which is constantly in a state of becoming, "God" brought forth order and endowed it with *soul* and *intelligence*. Thanks to the latter, 1) man can ascend to the realm of ideas on his own, 2) realize that they are the patterns by means of which the demiurge created everything else, and, thus, 3) base his life on their unending perfection, which are free of becoming and limitation.

Nowhere does Plato explain this better than in Book VII of the *Republic*. It follows Plato's Parable of the Cave, in which its prisoners are chained in such a way that they cannot see the objects behind them, but only the shadows of those objects cast by the light of a fire on a wall in front of them. Supposing the shadows to be real objects, they are misled until one of the prisoners is set free and dragged into the blinding light of the sun. Here he observers the sun's light, which illuminates the true world of observation, and which in turn opens the eyes of his mind to contemplate the highest "objects" of good. It is a slow and painful journey as one moves from the sensible world to the intellectual world of pure and beautiful forms. As Plato has Socrates explain:

> Every feature in this parable . . . is meant to fit our earlier analysis. The prison dwelling corresponds to the region revealed to us through the sense of light, and the fire-light within it to the power of the Sun. The ascent to see the things in the upper world you may take as standing for the upward journey of the soul into the region of the intelligible. . . . In the world of knowledge, the last thing to be perceived, and only with great difficulty, is the essential Form of Goodness. Once it is perceived, the conclusion must follow that, for all things, this is the cause of whatever is right and good; in the visible world it gives birth to light and to the lord of light, while it is itself sovereign in the intelligible world and the parent of intelligence and truth. Without having had a vision of this Form no one can act with wisdom either in his own life or in matters of state.[5]

Along with the *Timaeus*, *The Republic* is a masterpiece of intellectual ascent to the eternality of the Divine and its world of universals, attributing to God only that which is best, harmonious, and perfect.

Plato's pupil, Aristotle, took the argument the next step. In his *Metaphysics*, Aristotle establishes the distinction between actuality and

---

4. See Plato, *Timaeus*, 14.
5. See Abernethy and Langford, *History of Philosophy*, 51.

potentiality. Only that which possesses actuality can be the cause of anything potential, and, as with Plato, the artificer of the world would, therefore, have to possess pure actuality, free of any "becoming." In addition, as the universe's "artificer" he would have to be an "Unmoved Mover," inasmuch as if anything were to have moved him or move him he would not be the perfect all-encompassing *actus purus*. Since he neither needs nor desires anything apart from himself, he does not so much "create" the universe as the universe (as an existing *pleroma* of possibilities) moves itself. It does so in response to his perfection, desiring to be as much like him as possible. Similarly, as in the case of God, humankind's highest goal would be the contemplation of the highest perfection, which is reason in its purest form.[6]

In both Plato and Aristotle, God symbolizes the highest reality toward which mankind can aspire to achieve self-fulfillment. Aside from our ascent to God, or our participation in the noblest of ideas, we could never actualize our full potential. Our daily consciousness of this supreme Good is inseparable from our self-fulfillment. Once we lose sight of this highest Good, or God as its symbol, we lose sight of the mystery of our own potential, or of our own state of becoming, or its capacity to becoming fully actualized.

Aristotle also introduced a distinction between substance and accidents and universals and particulars. Everything that enjoys existence qualifies as a substance or possesses an innate form (like Plato's forms or ideas). But when a substance is individualized, or becomes a particular expression of a substance, its predicates may differ. The term "human being" refers to the formal substance that all humans possess. But each particular human possesses different predicates or accidents. Some are tall, some are short, some are wise, and some are foolish. Aristotle thought of universal substances as real referents, but not necessarily as entities enjoying a separate existence from thinking minds. These universal truths or formal substances are eternal, whereas individual states are limited and perishable. What is true of universals endures across time; whereas what is true of particulars will die in time. Universals, therefore, enjoy a superior essence over particulars.[7]

On the basis of this reasoning, one can see how later generations of Christian theologians were encouraged to define God in terms of God's unique substance, eternal and precedent, uncreated, without beginning

---

6. See Aristotle, *Metaphysics*, Book XII, chs. 5–7.
7. See Aristotle's *Prior Analytics* and *Posterior Analytics*.

or end, and thus the causal agent of everything contingent and becoming. Of necessity, God, the un-begotten had to exist for there to be anything begotten. Following this line of reasoning, St. Aquinas was able to 1) offer a series of rational proofs for the existence of God, as well as 2) provide a definition of God as eternal, infinite, wise, omnipotent, omniscient, and the formal essence of love itself. In all of this, Aquinas credits his conclusions to Aristotle's principles, which he gleaned from the latter's works.

Nonetheless, this way of reasoning from the individual to the universal and back down the steps of so lofty an ascent is a methodology based on the analytical and suppositional. It witnesses primarily to the genius of the human mind as it copes with itself and the universe. That the mind can arrive at a "that than which none greater can be conceived" belongs entirely within the power of the mind to transcend itself. There at the end of the ascent we arrive at a supposition that witnesses more to the truth about the self than about God. Within ourselves is a hunger to define that "Other" whom we encounter in our consciousness. It is a human who wrings from within her own depths what she cannot wring from the eternal, whether it is the result of a Dawkins meme, or of her inability to flee the presence of the Ineffable within. Such an artificer that reason posits satisfies that otherwise absurd climb up Sisyphus's hill without having to repeat the trek, day after day. No wonder Camus hypothesized that Sisyphus found his task "enjoyable," else human existence would sink below the value of the very stone it carries up the hill of mankind's destiny.

It was Philo of Alexandria, of Jewish heritage, who ventured the step of associating Plato's universal forms with the mind of God itself. For Plato and Aristotle, the universal forms co-existed with God and were employed by God (at least in Plato) in creating the universe. It cannot be ruled out, however, that Plato might have welcomed Philo's "clarification" of the placement of the *eideos* (ideas/forms) in God's mind, for how else may they be "contemplated" except by a mind? Nonetheless, for Philo, these universals are attributes of God, aspects of his divine nature, compatible with the Greek notions of reason, logos, and truth. In addition, he found them mirrored in the Ten Commandments and sacred wisdom of the Hebrew Bible. In other words, he located the forms or universals *in the divine mind* and not as ideas outside God's mind. When soon after Philo's time John's Gospel describes Christ as the Word of God, or states that "in the beginning was the logos, and the logos was with God, and the logos was God," and that "he was in the beginning with God . . . and became flesh and dwelt among us," we have nothing less than a restatement of Plato and Philo's philosophy, endorsed to interpret the enigmatic life of Jesus, in whom the very essence of God seemed to dwell.[8]

For this reason, one cannot rush to identify God with the noblest line of human thought. In truth it reveals more about our capacity of transcendence than it reveals about God. Until we understand and acknowledge the same, we are no better off than Plato's prisoners, bound facing their cave's wall, mistaking the shadows before them as the truth about the world.

Trapped also in this line of reasoning is the devaluation of the created order. The Hebrew Bible refuses to do this and pronounces creation "good." In drawing more on Greek thought than its own Old Testament roots, Christianity reshaped its concept of God and of God's universe along metaphysical lines rather than biblical insight. In a metaphorical sense, they exchanged the rose of Sharon for the beauty of a Grecian urn. The result was an era of asceticism foreign to its own lineage. Consequently, this bifurcation between time and eternity, the intellect and matter, was destined to require redress in the theologies of the period. How could the God of the universe, the un-begotten and not made, become flesh, live, suffer and die, subservient to the laws of perishable matter, unless born of a pure vessel, himself equal in *substance* with God and man, and resurrected into the heavenly realm again? Paul seems to have been under the sway of the Greek mind more than any of the Gospel writers, though John reflects this ambivalence in his contrast between spirit and flesh. Again, this should give us pause as we seek to enumerate the attributes of God.

Even reason is compelled to stop at the top of its ascent. The Old Testament reminds its most ardent believers that God can only be known on *God's* terms. God is what God is (Exod 3:6); his thoughts are not human thoughts, nor his ways human ways (Isa 55:8). Again, these are not God's words but the biblical writers'; nonetheless they witness to the limitations of reason. In the Old Testament, God remains ineffable. God stands apart from creation. He is known only insofar as he reveals himself directly (as in the case of Abraham), or via dreams (as in the case of Jacob). His law, revealed to Moses, becomes the normative principle for interpreting the rise and fall of Judah and Israel. Even though the psalmists' meditations are drawn largely from within the soul, yet they stand critiqued on the basis of the psalmists' interpretations of their people's faith. Psalm 119 is an excellent example of such a critique. In that respect, the psalmist is not unlike us,

---

8. See Philo, *De Oificio Mundi*, 1:9, 15, 115.

insofar as in our own involuntary moments of self-consciousness, when we sense the consciousness of that Other, we are equally mindful of the limitations of reason, lest we too hastily postulate that the "that than which none greater can be conceived" is equivalent to God. God will always exceed our definitions. In the Jewish and Christian scriptures, God remains mankind's final revealer of the highest truth. As essential as Plato's *nous* is, Christianity's biblical roots require the abasement of reason before the gates of Eternity. However, once the patristic theologians bent their knees to the God of Abraham, Isaac, and Jacob, they quickly snatched up Plato's forms again. In a nutshell, this constitutes Karl Barth's primary reason for rejecting any human ascent to know God. It is central to all fourteen of Barth's *Church Dogmatics*. Only God can reveal God. Humanity's *ratio* cannot achieve it.

If you have ever opened the *Bhagavad Gita*, or wandered down the pathways of Buddhism, you will encounter a similar humility before the Infinite. Vishnu in the descending guise of Krishna reminds his servant Arjuna of the mystery of that all-indwelling soul, which transcends reason while fulfilling life's journey through succeeding passages of time. So also the image of the Buddha comes to us. He is seated in silence before his followers, holding quietly nothing but the white blossom of the lotus in his lap. One must grasp with the eye of the soul what the spoken word cannot define. Did not even Jesus say: "Let him who has ears to hear listen"? Reason can only take us so far, though reason is our greatest gift. Little wonder that the Greeks raised monuments to Apollo, hailed Athena for her wisdom, and cherished Plato's "memoirs" of Socrates in his dialogues. They longed to use reason to understand what reason itself could not wholly disclose; that is, they overestimated the power of reason itself. Or little wonder that Shakespeare bemoaned man's dismissal of his Glassy Essence, which held his rational and appetitive natures in balance.

> [But] man, proud man,
> Drest in a little brief authority,—
> Most ignorant of what he's most assured,
> His glassy essence,—like an angry ape,
> Plays such fantastic tricks before high heaven
> As makes the angels weep . . . (*Measure for Measure* II.ii.)

The ancient world's fascination with the warring realms of mind and matter is reflected also in the writings of Plotinus. He too weaves together a story of ascent and descent, but in Plotinus' scheme, the One imparts its universals through the phenomenon of *emanation*. Emanating out from the One, as light emanates from the sun without diminishing it, graduations of being come into existence. First mind, then the world soul, next the human soul, and finally the world of matter. Each represents a diminution of perfection as the "light" shines farther and farther out from the "sun." In turn each emanation contains a higher and a lower order of being. As the mind looks toward the One, its level of existence enjoys a closer unity with God; but as the mind looks down toward the soul, its reality is diminished. This process of looking up versus looking down is true of all the levels of perfection, until, if one keeps looking down, one eventually comes to the darkest heart of matter, void of light and void of order. At this level, the soul in its downward glance, drawn so by its own material entrapment, encounters the realm of evil. When this hierarchy of perfection is reversed, and the soul rises above the body, and presses ever higher toward the One, unity with God is ultimately enjoyed, and salvation is obtained in the form of ecstatic union with the One.

A splendid example of Plotinus' reasoning abounds especially in his essay "On Beauty." Though somewhat convoluted and repetitive, he argues:

> For what can true self-control be except not keeping company with bodily pleasures, but avoiding them as impure and belonging to something pure? . . . Again greatness of soul is despising the things here: and wisdom is an intellectual activity, which turns away from the things below and leads the soul to those above. For one must come to the sight with a seeing power made akin and like to what is seen. . . . First the soul will come in its ascent to intellect and there will know the forms, all beautiful, and will affirm that these, the Ideas, are beauty.[9]

St. Augustine would absorb almost all of these elements into his theology of mankind's fall. While rejecting the idea of emanation, for Augustine, Adam's pride caused him to look away from God, and thus began his downward spiral into a life of ignorance, concupiscence, and death. Turning from his own earlier life of concupiscence, Augustine began his ascent to God, first through his devotion to Platonic thought, then through his discovery of Christ via Paul. Six centuries before Anselm, Augustine launched his own program of believing in order to understand, wedding his knowledge of scripture to the noblest of Platonic universals and virtues. He succumbed to the monastic life, somewhat a disdainer of the body, but his love of God,

---

9. Plotinus, *Enneads*, Vol. 1, 251–61.

combined with his quest for wisdom, produced a trove of magnificent works, his most enduring being his *Confessions* and *The City of God*. In many ways the latter is as Platonic a Christian tome as any a theologian has ever composed. As long as our eyes are fixed on the eternal city of God, the city of man does well; but once our gaze, our love, our glance turns to the soul's distracters, then the city of man declines in its perfection. All the ingredients of Plato and Plotinus inform its scope and structure. For this reason, Karl Barth—as hinted earlier—criticized Augustine's methodology of intellectual ascent, as it presumed a unity between God and man, which Barth's theological position rejected. (See Appendix B.)

Lastly in this brief survey, the writings of Pseudo-Dionysius the Areopagite deserve review. He too builds on Plotinus' doctrine of emanation, envisioning the world as a ladder of being, reaching upward to God while God's downward emanating light draws mankind upward to God. The gradation of things, or the great chain of being, is always and everywhere subservient to God's ordering of the created world. As in Aristotle and Plotinus, God is the *summum bonum*, the highest good that attracts, fulfills, and inspires human existence.

In addition, Dionysius maintained that God is best approached following two distinct ways, one positive and the other negative. As in Plato and Aristotle's systems, the *via positiva* ascribes to God the highest level of perfection, rendering his attributes free of all imperfection. Thus God becomes good, wise, one, and perfect in every way applicable to God. We, on the other hand, possess such attributes only in compromise. Of more significance, however, is the negative way, or *via negativa*. Dionysius was skeptical of our intellectual powers of ascent. Reasoning from this side of time to eternity, or from the individual and the finite to the infinite God of the universe struck him as risky. If God is perfect, how can he possess the characteristics of the less perfect? Thus Dionysius proposed denying aspects of creatureliness to God altogether. Consequently, God is best defined as *not being* material, perishable, moveable, divisible, begotten, becoming, impressionable, or changeable. In the end, God becomes unknowable by this method; indeed, ineffable.[10]

It was only the genius of Aquinas that salvaged this Dionysian method by reworking it in a more compelling theological way. He did so by offering a distinction between equivocal, univocal, and analogical use of language.

---

10. See Dionysius, *On Divine Names*, *Mystical Theology*, and *On the Heavenly Hierarchy* in the *Works of Dionysius*.

God's perfections are not utterly unlike or equivocal to ours, nor are they identical or univocal to ours. Rather, they are analogically related. What is appropriate to God's nature pertains to God and what is appropriate to ours pertains to us. Thus, Aquinas freed himself to use both the language of the classics and the language of scripture to develop his theology of the nature of God.[11] In the process, he built on the critical ideas of Dionysius while bringing out a more astute understanding of God's nature.

One could go on tracing the history of Platonic thought on Christian theology, but the quotes below from the 1959 revised edition of the Westminster Assembly's *Confession of Faith* confirm what has been demonstrated above.

First an influence from Plato, with a touch of Dionysius:

> There is but one only living and true God, who is infinite in being and perfection, a most pure spirit, invisible, without body, parts, or passions, immutable, immense, eternal, incomprehensible, almighty, most wise, most holy, most free, most absolute . . . (chapter two, I)

Then an influence from Aristotle:

> [Who] hath all life, glory, goodness, blessedness, in and of himself; and is alone in and unto himself all-sufficient, not standing in need of any creatures which he hath made, nor deriving any glory from them . . . (chapter two, II)

Two centuries following the original pronouncement of the Westminster Divines' 1648 *Confession of Faith*, the German philosopher Ludwig Feuerbach dismissed all such classical, scholastic, and Reformation theology as a tragic misunderstanding of man himself. All, all of it, he argued was caused by a sense of alienation that modern mankind felt in himself. Upon the screen of the infinite, man had projected his own sense of unworthiness, attributing to God what he had lost in himself. Thus seeing himself as finite, mortal, and broken, man was forced to look to God to regain and restore a liberated self. To be free and pure again, man had to reclaim for himself all that he had surrendered to God. For Feuerbach, it was time to bid farewell to the classical world and its religious man. A few of his trenchant thoughts are worth restating:

> [In] religion, consciousness of the object and self-consciousness coincide. The object of the senses is out of man, the religious object

---

11. See Aquinas, *Summa Contra Gentiles*, Vol. 1, chaps. 32–34.

is within him. . . . Consciousness of God is self-consciousness, knowledge of God is self-knowledge. . . . God is the manifested inward nature, the expressed self of a man. . . . The divine being is nothing else than the human being, or, rather the human nature purified, freed from the limits of the individual man, made objective—i.e., contemplated and revered as another, distinct being. All the attributes of the divine nature are, therefore, attributes of the human nature.[12]

How quickly others responded! Especially Nietzsche, who in his *Gay Science* and other iconoclastic pieces, strove to create an *Ubermensch*, a superior man, who needed neither God nor others to conquer the alienation his generation had inherited. In place of Plato's Parable of the Cave, Nietzsche offered his Mad Man's appearance in the public square to announce the "death" of God. Where now was mankind's Glassy Essence, if not shattered against the pavement stones where the Mad Man dashed his ghostly lantern?

More recently, a friendlier assessment of the classical attributes has been offered by Charles Hartshorne. In his *Omnipotence and Other Theological Mistakes*, Hartshorne criticized what he called the "six common mistakes about God" that need correcting.

According to Hartshorne, the tenets of classical theism "give the word God a meaning which is not true to its import in sacred writings or in concrete religious piety." He lists these mistakes: God is 1) absolutely perfect and therefore unchangeable; 2) omnipotent, 3) omniscient, 4) unsympathetic, 5) the guarantor of immortality, and 6) revealer of infallible truths. Hartshorne disagreed with all six. He did so on the basis of rejecting the Greek world's supposition concerning "change." Change for the Greek mind suggested weakness, imperfection, instability, and impermanence. But Hartshorne finds the classical world's definition of "perfect" to fail in describing the divine reality of either the Old or New Testament's witness to God. Granted, God may not be able to change for the worse, does it follow that every conceivable kind of change reflects "a fault or weakness"?[13] Only a definition that allows for growth, advancement, and positive good would be worthy of God's interaction with the world. Moreover, for Hartshorne, change does not have to result in destruction. Thanks to biology, physics,

---

12. Feuerbach, *Essence of Christianity*, quoted in Hick (ed.), *Classical and Contemporary Readings*, 149–50.

13. Hartshorne, *Omnipotence and Other Theological Mistakes*, 6.

and psychology, "creative becoming is no secondary, deficient form of reality."[14] The Greek universals were and are "abstract," whereas our lives are concrete and particular, at which level our interaction with God occurs. For any and all of this to happen, life has to be free; and God has to allow it to happen freely, without obstructing it by his omnipotence or ordaining it in accordance with his omniscience. In conclusion, Hartshorne argues: "Life simply is a process of decision making, which means that risk is inherent in life itself. Not even God could make it otherwise. A world without risks is not conceivable. At best it would be a totally dead world, with neither good nor evil."[15]

Throughout all of Hartshorne's analysis is his conviction that God is both in the world and above the world. He labels his view: "dual transcendence." The world is both a volitional and physical extension of God's engagement with life. He is involved in its processes both physically and spiritually.

> God is . . . both eternal and temporal in all surpassing ways; God alone has an *eternal individuality*, meaning unborn and undying, and God alone has enjoyed the entire past and will enjoy all the future. He-She is both physical and spiritual, and the divine body is all-surpassing and all-inclusive of the creaturely bodies, which are to God as cells to a supercellular organism. His-Her spirit embraces all the physical there is with all-surpassing, unstinted love.[16]

Far more could be said of this chapter's subject, but there remain other ways of defining God. To these we turn next.

---

14. Ibid., 8.
15. Ibid., 12.
16. Ibid, 44–45.

CHAPTER 3

The Ground of Being

PAUL TILLICH'S FAVORITE DESIGNATION for God was the phrase, "the Ground of Being." In Volume I of his *Systematic Theology*, he introduced the term in his discussion of "revelation." Revelation, he maintained, involves mystery, inasmuch as "it points to something which is essentially a mystery, something which would lose its very nature if it lost its mysterious character."[1] This occurs "when reason is driven beyond itself to its 'ground and abyss,' to that which 'precedes' reason, to the fact that 'being is and nonbeing is not' (Parmenides), to the original fact (*Ur-Tatsache*) that there is *something* and not *nothing*."[2] If this sounds like Aristotle's unmoved mover, or Plato's un-begotten demiurge who transcends and precedes all being, nonetheless, for Tillich, we are all "bearers of the mystery of being" and every thing "participates in being-itself," which is its ground and meaning. This is more than maintaining that God acts as the Unmoved Mover. God is the inescapable transcendent and immanent phenomenon underlying every entity and present in the "depths" of humankind's very mystery. A similar notion is also found in Plato's concept of the "Good," which is immanent in everything, according to each thing's participation in being.

In a more popular vein, Tillich addressed the above in terms of depth psychology. The latter leads us into levels of consciousness that uncover the hidden. But depth psychology alone "cannot guide us to the deepest

---

1. Tillich, *Systematic Theology*, I, 108.
2. Ibid., 110.

ground of our being and of all being, the depth of life itself," or to that "ground of all being," which is "God."

> That depth is what the word *God* means. And if that word has not much meaning for you, translate it, and speak of the depths of your life, of the source of your being, of your ultimate concern, of what you take seriously without any reservation. . . . For if you know that God means depth, you know much about Him.[3]

These quotes are taken from *The Shaking of the Foundations*. Specifically they are drawn from his chapter entitled, "The Depth of Existence," and are based on his exposition of the psalmist's words: "Out of the depths have I cried unto thee, O Lord" (Ps 130:1). The fact that God is the inexorable Ground of Being, or the depth we cannot flee (Ps 139), shifts the focal point from having to prove God as One who transcends and stands *outside* the universe to One who is known already from *within* the universe, indeed from within the self. Such an ontological argument may not prove the existence of God, but it witnesses to the mystery and depth of the self. God as the Ground of one's being carries with it a profound *existential* element that neither Plato's God of intellectual ascent nor Aristotle's Abstract Mover quite captures. (One qualification, however, does beg to be recognized: that for Plato the divine truth is *already present* in one, but unfortunately in a "forgotten" form.) From a critical perspective, as the "depths," the Ground of Being generates both an appeal and a peril: an appeal, insofar as God is within us, not outside of us, thus inseparable from our very sub-consciousness, which we grasp with immediacy—no ascent required; yet, a peril, inasmuch as the awareness of God as the Grounds fails to escape the stigma that it too is nothing more than epiphenomenal—a dimension of the way we think, feel, and fathom the self. Nonetheless, Tillich's "depths" makes it clear that one can distinguish between an intellectual *ratio* (reason) that fails to grasp God, versus one's existential *entis* (being) that already recognizes its inseparable unity—though flawed—with God.

It is from this respect, however, that an appreciation of other religions can be established. There too—in Hinduism, Buddhism, and many other religions—the awareness of "God" as the ground of Being is experienced in one's "depths." That revelatory moments and sacred insights may differ is of far less consequence than the experience of the depths of the Ground of Being. That is why a religion that spurns the "trans-global" reality of

---

3. Tillich, *Shaking of the Foundations*, 57.

others' experiences does an injustice to any analysis of the God question. As the Ground of Being, God is the depths present in all religions and in all religious and non-religious people.

In Whitehead's mind, however, the idea of the "depths" runs the risk of an "extreme doctrine of immanence." In his view it contains elements of pantheism, too. At the time Whitehead was writing, he categorized Hinduism and Buddhism as representative of "impersonal concepts of God," or concepts of "an impersonal order to which the world conforms."[4]

While it is true that in Hinduism, Brahman, the impersonal and unrevealed source of all mystery, is unknowable and ineffable, it is also true that Brahman manifests itself in highly personal and knowable forms. The many deities that comprise India's religious culture are personal and tangible dimensions of the abstract Brahman. Two deities in particular stand out as personal manifestations of the transcendent-yet-ever-immanent Brahman—namely, Vishnu and Shiva. It is instructive to explore this dual dimension of Brahman, inasmuch as it illuminates the Eastern understanding of God as the Ground of Being.

The Hindu scholar Nikhilananda elucidated the above with sufficient clarity in his writings. In his translation of the *Upanishads*, Nikhilananda explains that the sole purpose of the commentaries is to prove the reality of Brahman and the unreality of the universe of names and forms. Their purpose is to establish the absolute oneness of the embodied soul (yours and mine) with Brahman.[5] Whereas more popular Hindu scriptures, such as the Vedas, offer colorful stories, religious poetry, and information about Brahman, on the contrary, the texts of the *Upanishads* encourage existential knowledge of Brahman. They elicit a more austere, disciplined, and concentrated effort to *experience* the all-pervasive character of Brahman. The intention or goal is for the seeker to become aware of his "deeper phases of existence" until aware of and one with the imperishable reality, Brahman. It is often expressed as "That Thou art." Any differentiations between the self and God are obliterated—an end not unlike what Plotinus and Augustine might have favored. If this sounds like monism, there are safeguards against it.

Risking oversimplification, Nikhilananda explains that the *Upanishads* teach the truth about three things: 1) living beings (*jivas*), 2) the universe, and 3) God. Concerning the latter, the *Upanishads* describe the nature and

---

4. Whitehead, *Religion in the Making*, 66
5. Nikhilananda, *Upanishads*, 25.

attributes of Brahman, its reality, manifestations, powers, and aspects. This knowledge is essential to the soul, as "man is rooted in a reality far deeper than is apparent to the senses. Just as a small portion of an iceberg is visible, so only a small portion of man is available to the senses."[6] In Nikhilananda's view, the sages of the *Upanishads* described Brahman as having two aspects, one devoid of qualities; the other endowed with qualities; the former designated as Nirguna Brahman, the latter as Saguna Brahman. For Nikhilananda, Nirguna Brahman best captures the nature of God. In his mind "IT" and "THAT" come closest to describing the impersonal properties of Brahman. As the Hindu THAT than which none greater can be conceived, the way of negation produces the following attributes: "unperceived, incomprehensible, un-inferable, and indescribable."[7] Nikhilananda considered Nirguna Brahman's most salient feature as "pure consciousness" void of any content. It is consciousness itself, the essence of consciousness, illuminating everything.

As the eternal THAT, Brahman, as consciousness, cannot be worshipped, prayed to, or meditated upon. THAT is not an object of reflection; rather IT is "the intangible Unity that pervades all relative existence."[8] God as Nirguna Brahman "is the immortal essence of every human being." In Tillichian terms, Nirguna Brahman is the equivalent of the Ground of Being, or, in more colloquial terms, each of us is a manifestation of God, or a conscious extension of God in space and time. What prevents this from lapsing into monism is the dynamic nature of each "*jiva*," or "life," which is comprised of individualized and unique layers of sensations and feelings, thoughts and actions, in which the One reality, Brahman—central for all existence—remains when all else passes away. It is like the Old Testament's *ru'ah*, or God's breath, which returns to God when man's *athama*, or mortal frame, returns to dust.

We can understand why Whitehead labeled "this Eastern Asiatic concept" the "extreme doctrine of immanence."

It is only when we leave the *Upanishads* and come to the *Bhagavad Gita* that we encounter God's personal side in the form of Saguna Brahman, or God with qualities. Hinduism supports the human need to know God at a personal level. In Hindu thought, God has revealed himself as knowable and approachable, as One to whom devotees may pray and on whom they

6. Ibid., 29.
7. Ibid., 33.
8. Ibid., 39.

may meditate. This is especially so with respect to Saguna Brahman, who reveals himself in the form of India's triune deities of Brahma (Creation), Vishnu (Preservation), and Shiva (Dissolution), each of whom supports the human need for illumination, encouragement, and purpose. Nevertheless, Nirguna Brahman, as the immanent Ground of Being, is never far away. Nowhere is this better celebrated in the *Bhagavad Gita* than in Vishnu's descent in the form of the Lord Krishna, as he comforts his servant Arjuna. As the latter's chariot sweeps the young prince into battle, Krishna says:

> Never have I not existed, nor you, nor these kings; and never in the future shall we cease to exist.... [The] embodied self is enduring, indestructible, and immeasurable.... It is not born; it does not die; it will never cease to be; unborn, enduring, constant, and primordial. It is not killed when the body is killed.[9]

This reality is our Ground of Being. Vishnu is in us and we are in Vishnu.

Buddhism would carry this a step further. In Buddhism, the key is to wake up as the Buddha did, and see things as they are: that everything is interrelated, that the conscious ego is part and parcel of everything else. To think that I am separable from everything and everyone else is an illusion. Even when I enter my own consciousness, I never actually meet a "self" that isn't attached to some shifting emotion, elusive memory, or changing thought and mood. Where is there any separate self? Rather, I belong to something all encompassing, ever changing, ever impermanent, a *tathata*, a suchness that defines us all. That is our Ground of Being. And it leads to *Sunya*, or emptiness—the realization that we need to extinguish that "false self" within our consciousness and see things as they are. Such brings great peace and freedom. It is a facet of Buddhist "mindfulness" (i.e., of letting go of things that detract from one's being in the moment), and therefore unavailable to the Buddha Essence and others. That doesn't mean that we cease to care about ourselves or others, only that we may now do so from a wider and more tolerant perspective.[10]

Closely linked is Jesus' own insistence that we must be born anew; that he who seeks to save his life will lose it, but whoever loses his life for Christ and the gospel's sake will find it. Even more powerful is Jesus' statement: "In that day you will know that I am in the Father and I in you and you in me" (John 14:20). The likelihood that Jesus was schooled in Brahmanic

---

9. Cited by R. E. Van Voorst in *Anthology of World Scriptures*, 55.
10. See Christian Humphreys' discussion of the above in *Buddhism*, 148–49.

or Buddhist thought is doubtful, but the similarity between each religion's experiences of the "depths" is unmistakable.

This brings us back to Hartshorne and Whitehead and their process philosophy. For both, God is involved in the world. God is affected by the world and its concurrences. Because God interacts with the world, his knowledge of and closeness to the world changes God. In other words, it adds to his experiences of the world and us. This is due to the fact that God is a living God and not an abstract metaphysical principle. When Hartshorne speaks about God's "dual transcendence," he means that while God is involved in the world, God still enjoys an *eternal essentiality*, which is unchanging amid the world's processes and changes. God is not to be identified with the world, as in pantheism, yet God is in the world, shaping it in novel ways. We are part of that novelty with all the risks and possibilities it provides. Indeed, both God and we are evolving, but we are evolving in the direction that God's eternal essentiality moves us. Indeed, God's purpose "is the attainment of value in the temporal world."[11]

Upon first glance, it may not appear that there is any unity between Tillich's Ground of Being and Hinduism's Nirguna Brahman, let alone the Buddha's realization that we are each an inseparable facet of a universal process. But when viewed from Hartshorne's perspective, all three share the insight that we are living, evolving components of an Eternal reality that underlies all that we are. It is our "depths." We are the living manifestation of its reality and presence, if not the glassy mirror of God "himself."

The depths speak of immediacy. God is already present as that than which none closer can be experienced. God's existence is existential, unmediated, felt with an inner assurance that reason can neither explain nor dispel. In this scenario, God becomes the calm unity of an existential presence that links the all with the all, or that Brahmanic essence experienced as the Buddhist emptiness that overflows with bliss and enlightenment. Such consciousness is already God-consciousness even if one is not immediately conscious of God. Though elements of Christianity might balk at the thought, mankind becomes a plethora of facemasks that God wears with glory and joy, preserving each player's identity in the eternal gallery of God's theatre of unforgettable love.

As the Ground of Being, God further qualifies as the essence of hope and love. These attributes are elements of our depths in addition to discoveries of intellectual ascent. The self knows it needs both hope and love.

---

11. Whitehead, *Religion in the Making*, 97.

THE GROUND OF BEING

It escapes into itself to find both when others turn against it. The cry for mercy is the recognition of an alienation that the self knows must be overcome. Not finding redemption outside the self, it finds it within its depths, where unity with God reassures and consoles the soul. "Be still and know that I am God" is not so much the product of intellectual ascent as it is the insight of a contrite heart. In Whitehead's view, this represents our advancement from "God the enemy to God the companion."[12] God the enemy is the God who must be placated, to whom sacrificial and guilt offerings must be provided. "He" is the God whose commandments must be observed and whose taboos must be acknowledged. "He" is the God of the communal and mythical stage of religion, not that of the individual in his/her solitariness. The God of companion eclipses the God of vengeance and reprimand. We see the transition in Samuel's famous lines: "Surely to obey is better than sacrifice and to heed than the fat of rams" (1 Sam 15:22). It is only in John's Gospel and letters that God the companion finally makes it onto the stage as Love. "God is love, and those who abide in love abide in God, and God in them" (1 John 4:16). Love is the Ground of Being, of all being, giving, shaping, and interacting with all that becomes and passes away into God again.

A similar transition occurred in Hinduism, which is traceable in the *Rig Veda*. There the gods are manifestations of the mystery of being, each an aspect of the created universe. Some are sky gods, others gods of the air, and still others gods and goddesses of the earth. Among the sky gods who best reveal this process of individuation are Savitar and Dawn. Savitar, the sun god, brings blessings daily to all his devotees who bask in the warm rays of his light and of whom it is proclaimed: "chases from us all distress and sorrow" (Hymn XXXV). So too Dawn: "who hath awakened every living creature. . . . Foe-chaser . . . protectress, joy-giver, waker of all pleasant voices" (Hymn CXIII).[13]

To be certain, a pantheistic element undergirds the *Rig Veda*'s gods and goddesses, as they are inseparable from the creation's cycles. They are grounded in the very essence of its mystery, by means of which God's goodness flows with abundance into mankind's life. Nonetheless, the interaction between Savitar and his devotees or Dawn and her worshippers enables the latter in each case to experience a calming beneficence amid life's harrowing

---

12. Whitehead, *Religion in the Making*, 16.
13. See the *Rig Veda*, in Griffith's *Sacred Writings: Hinduism*.

tenure. In this transition, God becomes less of a Brahmanic IT and more of a benevolent THOU.

In conclusion, God as the Ground and Depths of Being implies a set of propositions that deserve mention. Drawing upon the above discussion, it is possible to define God as:

1. Thou without whom nothing would exist.
2. Thou apart from whom nothing can exist.
3. Thou because of whom all persist,
4. Thou of whom all consist:
    (a) as cellular extensions of divine volition and
    (b) conscious dimensions of divine immanence.

The notion that the divine is within us may seem alien to the modern mind. However, perhaps it is not as strange to us as it at first appears. Consider the Jewish Kabbalist idea about divine sparks. According to Kabbalist belief, when God created the universe, it contained so much of his glory that it exploded into a zillion sparkling sacred shards. Consequently, all created entities contain fragments of these glowing hints of God. In modern terms, the shards are elements of quantum physics, those electromagnetic particles that form the nucleus of every atomic wave and particle that underlies our beingness. In that sense we are the physical extension of God's glory and mystery. He is in us and we are in him. We carry his *I Am* to the day we return to the elemental mix from whence we've come.

In a more poetic vein, one might define God as the consciousness of the universe, or as the creative force that comes to consciousness in all living things at whatever stage of sentience their natures are capable of manifesting. In inanimate objects, God is present in the very molecular structure of their elemental being by virtue of God's creative and life-sustaining élan. In animate subjects, he is present in their multiple levels of awareness, however faint or magnificent they may rise to glory—from the lowliest bacteria to the trumpeting elephant and ferocious tiger; from the tiniest songbird to the largest rollicking sea-sporting whale. In human beings, God's presence soars to the heights of humanity's unbounded imagination, energy, endeavor, and will. As conscience and redeemer, God guides man to the loftiest pinnacle of his self-fulfillment, gracing him with the gifts of transcendence, mercy, faith, and love.

CHAPTER 4

Language, Truth, and Metaphor

THE BASIC PURPOSE OF language is to allow persons to communicate with each other. What they communicate depends on their interests and/or needs. To achieve this, a variety of statement forms may be employed. Every field of human endeavor utilizes a language appropriate to its ends and purposes. This is as true of religion as it is of science, art, medicine, mathematics, and ethics.

Philosophers prefer to speak of "propositions" rather than sentences, as forms of the latter do not always impart useful information. For example, exclamations, prayers, explanations, and commands qualify as non-propositional sentences—they are not the kind of speech act of which one can ask, "Is that true or false?" They don't impart any information, and are thus not open to either verification or falsification. Even theologians have been forced to acknowledge their past emphasis on propositions and to recognizing the importance of both propositional *and* non-propositional statements. The former enunciate and clarify theological beliefs; whereas non-propositional statements may express responses to divine-human encounters, or one's experience of enlightenment, however achieved or induced. Not all language is about passing on factual data. And this is true not only at the level of the sentence, but also at the level of larger expanses of language. Here we can distinguish different genres, which can serve very different ends. One may think, for instance, of the form of legend, saga, lament, parable, poem, myth, drama, or first-person narrative. Theological beliefs may be embedded but not emphasized explicitly. Any intended instruction or insight is for the reader or listener to infer. It is the encounter that matters, the sense of awareness and fulfillment that counts, the feeling of divine presence or self-awakening to life's deeper truths that is aroused. Propositional statements require critical defense and logical validity, whereas non-propositional statements or genres that are not restricted to stating empirical facts witness to personal and spiritual insight. In the final analysis, the latter can make glad the heart of the religious person just as much as, or even more than, the former. They become the shining lamps that guide one's heart to the truth.

For philosophical empiricists, only those propositions that convey information about experiences that can be replicated or verified qualify as truth-statements. They alone describe the kind of world in which we live, and they alone can be tested as true or false. Since the time of Immanuel Kant, two principal types of propositions (defined as early as Aristotle) have attracted philosophical attention: analytic and synthetic statements. Analytic statements are propositions arrived on the basis of *necessity* and *universality*.[1] For Kant, judgments are either derived from experience (a posteriori) or

> are independent of experience and even of all impressions of the senses. Such knowledge is entitled a priori, and distinguished from the empirical, which has its sources a posteriori, that is, in experience.[2]

Furthermore, analytic statements are said to contain the meaning of their propositions within themselves, or, their predicates are already included in their subject nouns. The noun "men" in the statement "all men are mortal" already contains its predicate within the subject, since we know that to be human is to be finite and mortal. Therefore, of *necessity* and universally, I, for example, am compelled to conclude that, since I am a man, I am mortal, and must die. As such, analytical statements do not impart any new information or add to our storehouse of knowledge. Nonetheless, in science, such analytical statements, derived after ample experimentation and replication of synthetic judgments have been tested, may legitimately form axiomatic statements that can be used in creating theories, or as premises for rational arguments. For example: "A blue litmus paper will turn red when dipped in an acidic solution; whereas a red paper will turn blue under alkaline conditions."

---

1. Kant, *Critique of Pure Reason*, 377.
2. Ibid., 376.

It is only when we come to synthetic statements that we encounter "existential import." The latter means that a proposition's subject truly exists in reality and its predicates are the legitimate result of observation and reason. "This songbird has a brown, black, and white breast" is an example of a synthetic statement. When raised to the level of an analytic statement, it could mean; "All tow-he's have brown, black, and white breasts." "Jesus wept" is likewise a synthetic statement, although we only have one ancient document to "verify" it in John 11:35. Nonetheless, theologians have seized on this synthetic passage to argue that Jesus was fully human, a proposition of paramount value in the early church's struggle against Gnosticism. Consequently, the synthetic proposition "Jesus wept" bolstered the church's claim—based on other similar passages—that, as fully human, Jesus represented all humanity on the cross, thereby establishing a propositional statement of dogma.

Many of today's philosophers denigrate religious statements of either kind as imparting any genuine information about the universe. Kant did as much himself, arguing that subjects such as God and the soul cannot be derived synthetically, but only as transcendental judgments based on the mind's operations to seek unity. In unison with Kant, many of today's philosophers argue that only scientific statements, based on research, observation, and/or mathematical calculation provide authentic knowledge about the world. The truth or falsehood of such propositions can be tested again and again, as well as serve as premises for new theories. Since religious statements cannot be verified, they are said to contain no cognitive or representative value. The American philosopher John Randall espouses this view, arguing that scientific statements alone qualify as "cognitive" and "representative." As such, scientific statements contribute to our "factual knowledge" of the universe as well as "represent" actual entities "out there." On the other hand, religious statements are entirely "non-cognitive" and "non-representative" and thus provide zero information about the real entities that comprise the universe. Their only value is one of "insight." At best they provide a kind of *savoir-faire*, or know-how as to enhance one's personal life. But they cannot tell us how the world was created or what its purpose might be, or whether God exists, or an afterlife awaits us beyond this one.[3]

---

3. See John Randall's *Role of Knowledge in Western Religion*, in Hick, *Classical and Contemporary Readings*, 313–33.

Now, unlike Randall, I do think that there is a cognitive dimension to some religious language. Nevertheless, he is right to stress the value of non-cognitive religious speech. Indeed, it can be argued that non-cognitive religious language possesses a function that links us to our very being—indeed, the Ground of Being. Nowhere is this more implicit than in Martin Heidegger's *Poetry, Language, Thought*. Granted, his essay carries us into the realm of psychology and poetry; nonetheless, it is a brilliant commentary on our essential "beingness" as a manifestation of the Ground of Being. Heidegger's concern is that the modern era has reduced us to objectifications of technology. Instead of embracing our continuity with nature as our ground of Being, we have used technology to replace nature with an assertive will that is itself a function of technology. Consequently, we have contributed to our own "default" as human beings and have lost our sense of identity and direction. Certainly, reducing ourselves to entities for whom empirically testable synthetic statements alone define truth and falsehood, and for whom non-propositional statements of the heart have zero value, tends to devalue any human sense of wonder and worth as manifestations of the mystery of Being.

Heidegger advances his argument by means of a metaphysical interpretation of Hölderlin's famous poem, "Bread and Wine." The line that captures Heidegger's attention has to do with the need for what poets do "in a destitute time," as well as the poet's answer: "But they are . . . like the wine god's priests," traveling "from land to land in holy night." We live in a destitute time, because since the great god-men of the classical world have left the world, "the evening of the world's age has been declining toward its night." All this has created "the default of God." This does not mean, however, that our relationship with God has to be viewed negatively. Writes Heidegger:

> The default of God means that no god any longer gathers men and things unto himself, visibly and unequivocally, and by such gathering disposes the world's history and man's sojourn in it. The default of God forebodes something even grimmer, however. Not only have the gods . . . fled, but the divine radiance has become extinguished in the world's history. The time of the world's night is the destitute time, because it becomes ever more destitute.[4]

That is why the poets, acting as Dionysus's priests, keep the possibility of our true nature alive by singing the wine god's song "in holy night." Indeed,

---

4. Heidegger, *Poetry, Language, Thought*, 89.

even the destitute time of the world's night is still a "holy night," pregnant with the possibility of mankind's discovering his true self again. As we shall see, however, in chapter 12, Heidegger's *poetical use of language* to define the human condition and God, is roundly rejected by Martin Buber. Why? Because any "truth" based on metaphor is a human projection and not an authentic encounter with God as the One who stands outside and over against man. Nevertheless, as Hartshorne has aptly pointed out: "any idea of God must in some way make use of analogies, or at least metaphors, in attempting to show how our idea of the radically superhuman can nevertheless be our human idea."[5] Did not Aquinas make use of the same in his distinction between analogical, equivocal, and univocal uses of language?

Philosophers recognize a variety of theories concerning "truth." Three in particular deserve recognition. First, is the "correspondence theory," which maintains that propositions are true if they actually represent genuine facts that are "out there." For example, the Big Bang theory, though still a theory, corroborates the best knowledge we have amassed concerning the origin of the universe: *that it began with a big bang*. The Big Bang theory is true, if it is true, if and only if it corresponds to reality external to us, to *what actually happened*. That Homo sapiens arrived late on the planet Earth also fits in with this theory, as the research of anthropologists and paleontologists seems to prove that humankind did not evolve until several million years ago. Those are facts about mankind—out there to be discovered—and not simply feelings about man's origin.

A second theory of truth is known as the "coherence theory." It holds that if a known entity behaves in a certain way while a corresponding unknown entity's behavior cannot be determined it is likely that the unknown entity behaves in a similar way. More specifically, it argues that a proposition is true if and only if it coheres with other propositions within an already-accepted inter-connected set of propositions. For example, mankind knew what the exposed surface of the moon looked like, but no one could see its dark side. Nonetheless it was assumed to be similar to its sun-lit side. Then, once satellites and astronauts were able to orbit the moon, it was clearly established that its dark side was similar in structure and quality to its illuminated face. David Hume invoked the coherence theory in his refutation of "natural theology," in which he argued that "like events require only like causes." On this basis he declined to believe in a Creator of the universe as championed by the church and natural theology proponents of his era.

---

5. Hartshorne, *Omnipotence*, 54.

A third popular theory is known as the "pragmatic theory." The American philosopher William James espoused this view, especially in his monumental work *The Variety of Religious Experience*. He concluded that if a belief makes a difference for the better in how we act or think then it has "cash value." If it works, or is practical, embrace it. On this grounds, he found religion to be both "philosophically reasonable" and of immense psychological and spiritual comfort.[6]

Of these acknowledged theories, the correspondence and coherence theories perhaps best serve religious interests by providing confident sources of justification for one's beliefs, etc. The coherence theory works well since it is in the "depths" of our self-consciousness that we encounter the Ground of Being, thus allowing us to experience an awareness of that which is similar to but far more ultimate than our personal self. It underlies Aquinas' *analogia entis* principle, or his emphasis on our analogical relationship with God, in which what is appropriate to our being enables us to postulate, if not find affinity with, what is appropriate regarding God's being. More than a metaphor, God is the reality for which only poetic metaphor best attests. Once we embrace God as the Ground of Being, it is possible to discover our happiest identity, as the "default of God" melts away. In many respects, Heidegger's "default of God" is comparable to Whitehead's "God the void," and once the transition from "God the void" to "God the enemy" is complete, we are renewed and redeemed by "God the companion." As the psalmist expressed in his own words:

> Whither shall I go from thy Spirit?
> Or whither shall I flee from thy presence?
> If I ascend to heaven, thou art there!
> If I make my bed in Sheol, thou art there! . . .
> How precious to me are thy thoughts, O God!
> How vast is the sum of them! (Ps 139)

Within the range of all three theories, metaphor becomes both a poetic and psychological venue for applying and exploring "religious truth." Though such "truth" can never be proven true or false on the basis of logic or theories of linguistic analysis, metaphor enables the heart to embrace the God who encounters man in the deeper levels of the self. As the Lord Krishna put it: "never has there been a time when you did not exist." Metaphor enables the soul to articulate the belief that God has forever

---

6. James, *Variety of Religious Experience*, 33.

carried mankind in his heart. No matter how "non-cognitive" and "non-representative" religious propositions may be, they speak to the depths of the human condition beyond the power of empirical language to address. This does not denigrate the value of scientific propositions whatsoever. The Big Bang and Evolution are indispensable to our understanding of the universe's origin and our own evolution as primates with incredible gifts. At the same time, scientific discoveries in no way undermine the phenomenon of the heart's self-conscious awareness of its Ground of Being. Whether we call that phenomenon "God," "That Thou art," "Brahman," or the "Buddha essence" is secondary to our recognition of the grandeur of Being, which bears us forward toward its unknown destiny. There is no clash here between science and religion; rather both constitute complementary ways of recognizing the same reality, though relating to it in different ways.

In light of the hard "facts" of science, it behooves religious followers to adopt a theologically honed language that utilizes responsible metaphors vis-à-vis existence. Nothing is to be gained by denying the "facts" of the universe, which define our very existence. Rather, theological metaphor allows us to apply the "insight" of our encounters with life's depths to engage in the universe's larger story of evolution and development. We can become integral facets of that forward novelty or remain in the "default" of our own "night."

When religious language is true to itself, it provides humanity with interpretive powers by means of which we can express our encounter with Being. It is the language of response, not merely a language of feelings or aesthetics. One could list a score of purposes that a metaphorical approach proffers, but the following have proven beneficial.

Ontological. *Ontos* has to do with being, with reality as it impinges upon us. Religious myth, metaphor, and poetry enable us to respond to the unconditional demands and dilemmas of life as it is. As Job put it, "man is born to trouble as the sparks fly upward" (Job 5:7). Religious language provides insight for wrestling with life's uncompromising ways and to do so with integrity and wisdom. Rather than wasting away in one's morbid subjectivity, religious language provides an interpretive path that undergirds one's leap of faith rather than weakening it.

Existential. Religious language is existential. Life is filled with "real" and "unavoidable" troubles, opportunities, and possibilities. Many of these are urgent, inescapable, and replete with anxiety. Life's issues seize us; they possess immense import. Religious metaphors empower us to overcome the existential ironies of existence and conquer our ever-recurring fears. "You grieve for those beyond grief, and you speak words of insight," Krishna whispers to Arjuna, "but learned men do not grieve for the dead or the living" (*Bhagavad-Gita*, chapter 2, 55). Or as Jesus phrased it: "Leave the dead to bury the dead" (Luke 9:60). Life is filled with challenges and opportunities that far outweigh fear and anxiety. Our task is to face life's uncertainties with vitality and courage. Pausing to look back in weakness rather than accepting life's worst, prevents us from moving forward, and thus serves to no avail.

Aretetical. Aristotle seized upon *arête* (excellence) in his *Nicomachean Ethics*. He did so to advance his injunctions concerning personal and civil excellence. To do the right thing at the right time in the right way for the right reason results in "excellence," a sense of virtue that deepens one's character and integrity. It is a virtue that ennobles the self as much as it does the state. Religious stories, sagas, psalms, and metaphor offer invaluable stimuli for achieving a life defined by *arête*, or excellence.

Therapeutic. Religious insights, legends, and parables provide deep therapeutic catharsis for the sore bestead, lonely, and dying. "Today you will be with me in paradise" undergirds our mortal pilgrimage with quiet calm. It steels us with assurance that our lives are unique, never to be repeated by anyone else, nor ever able to "unbecome," in Hartshorne's words.

Regulative. One of Kant's favorite terms was "regulative." He used it in conjunction with his theory of "transcendental ideas." As a good philosopher, he reasoned that what we know are phenomena (or things as they appear to us) but not "things-in-themselves." Sensory perception provides our brains with numerous sensory data, but the mind imposes on all that data its own categories in order to make sense of the world. Kant did not doubt the "reality" of the data that comes to the mind before being processed. Just because the mind cannot know "things in themselves," or noumena, does not mean that the world outside our minds does not exist. He rejected such an extreme form of idealism, such as George Berkeley endorsed, according to which there is no mind-independent reality. However, ideas like God and the self transcend sensory data. To deduce them the mind has to postulate a higher order of the disparate experiences that comprise our lives. For example, to make sense of the many fleeting moments of consciousness we experience, we are compelled to posit a continuous self in whom the fleeting representations occur, thus our sense of self-consciousness as a self is preserved. The same for God, whom we postulate in order to justify our sense of duty and reward. In no case is the self or God an "illusion." The datum of life is required to prompt our needed transcendental ideas to do justice to life's experiences. In turn, it led Kant to postulate his famous Categorical Imperative that commands everyone to treat his neighbor as an end and not as a means only. Regulative ideas do not comprise the world (i.e., they possess neither cognitive nor representative information), as Randall might argue; nonetheless they enable us to regulate our lives in meaningful and worthwhile ways. This is especially true of the moral order, as Kant's Categorical Imperative makes clear.

Every religion is filled with Kant's phenomenon of the regulative function of the transcendent, especially in the realm of ethics. "Thou shalt not bear false witness" [Judaism and Christianity]; "To eliminate suffering, one must eliminate craving" [Buddhism]; "perform the duty unique to your caste with single minded devotion and you will experience karma at its best" [Hinduism]; "Gateless is the Great Tao; there are thousands of ways to it. If you pass through this barrier, you may walk freely in the universe" [Zen]. Such regulative injunctions are vital to man's sojourn as he seeks to make sense of the galactic splendor he calls the "universe." It enables him to accept his place in it with meaning and joy as he passes through its inviting gateways.

Having said all this, however, one must bear in mind Buber's concern for poetic language. Poetry is a human response. It is a facet of our self-consciousness, or subjectivity. For Buber, God exists beyond our objectifications of God as well as our subjective encounters with God. If God is no more than an extension of our language, a metaphor of our interiority, then such a God is not the God of biblical faith or Western metaphysics.[7] Again, also, Kant's warning about noumena deserves reiteration. Though we may never be able to know an "object in itself," that does not mean that the object is an "illusion." As Kant explains:

> When I say that the intuition of outer objects and the self-intuition of the mind alike represent the objects and the mind, that is, as they appear, I do not mean to say that these objects are a mere *illusion*. For in an appearance the objects, nay even the properties that we ascribe to them, are always regarded as something actually given.[8]

---

7. See Buber, *Eclipse of God*, 28.
8. Kant, *Critique of Pure Reason*, 393.

CHAPTER 5

A Critique of the Philosophical Arguments for the Existence of God

IN THE PRECEDING CHAPTERS, Anselm's ontological argument has been presented and references to Thomas Aquinas' cosmological argument mentioned. Aside from Anselm's argument, however, Aquinas' impressive five arguments for God's existence have not been critiqued in any detail. It is time to do so.

His first three are versions of the cosmological argument, his fourth a form of the moral argument, and fifth is a teleological argument, or argument from design. In many respects, the first three are strictly philosophical arguments, based on the methodology of intellectual ascent, inspired by Plato and Aristotle's works. They begin with effects and argue to the highest cause possible, beyond which no greater logical cause can be posited. The emphasis falls upon logic. The moral and teleological arguments, however, represent more subtle approaches. One may even call them non-propositional arguments, insofar as their inspiration is subjective and emotive. How one feels about the good and the beautiful (the moral argument) or how one views purpose and meaning (design) replaces the cold march of pure logic. In fact, the teleological argument includes both purpose and aesthetics, as design is a derivative of beauty.

First, however, Aquinas' Five Ways require a brief footnote to understand his introductory objections to Anselm's ontological argument. Though Aquinas does not mention Anselm by name, he repeats Anselm's line about that "than which nothing greater can be conceived." What he disliked about Anselm's argument was the latter's proposition that man's knowledge of God is self-evident. The only thing that is self-evident, for Aquinas, is the *idea* of God, which contains within itself the requirement of God's necessary existence. But this does not constitute a *proof* in Aquinas' mind. It only posits God in the broadest sense, still confining God to subjectivity. As he writes: "To know that God exists in a general and confused way is . . . not to know absolutely that God exists."[1] The proposition that God exists "needs to be demonstrated by things that are more known to us, though less known in their nature—namely, by His effects."[2] Thus, Aquinas proceeds to his Five Ways, all of which commence with known effects, using logic to lift the believer to the primal truth implied in the effects. In Aquinas' mind, to know *that* God exists can be demonstrated in this way (from effects to cause); nonetheless, in the final analysis, to know *who* God is can only be fleshed out in Scripture.

The first argument of the cosmological series is the argument from motion. Anything in motion has to have been placed in motion by something prior to it, which in turn requires a moving force to have set it in motion. Borrowing from Aristotle's distinction between potentiality and actuality, only that which is actually in motion can change the state of something possessing potentiality. "For motion is nothing else than the reduction of something from potentiality to actuality."[3] Note that the underlying issue here has to do with "change" or transformation. For Aristotle, an existent agent had to precede another agent's transition toward its final fulfillment. The Greek world was fascinated by the phenomenon of change as well as impermanence and an entity's highest good. Aquinas freely incorporates Aristotle's language of "potentiality" and "actuality" to argue that only an agent that possesses complete actuality in itself and requires nothing to set it in motion can logically bring this series of "change" to a happy conclusion. That entity of pure actuality is therefore the mover of all other motion, and thus rightfully may be called God. It represents St. Thomas' counterpart to Aristotle's Unmoved Mover and Plato's divine Craftsman without beginning.

His second argument is from the nature of efficient causation. Once more, he is incorporating Aristotle's notion of a required primary cause to produce a secondary cause. For Aquinas, nothing can boast of being its own

---

1. See Hick, *Classical and Contemporary Readings*, 38.
2. Ibid.
3. Ibid., 41.

cause. Everything owes its existence to a preceding agent; if not, it would be self-caused, or prior to itself, which is impossible. There must be a first cause to account for intermediate causes, which in turn enable other agents to reach their final causes. Without this first cause, neither intermediate nor final causes, nor their effects, would exist. Note again Aristotle's language of efficient cause and final cause, which brings about a thing's highest good. If we take away the first cause, or primal cause, which enjoys its highest purpose in itself and requires no preceding cause for its own existence, then no efficient, intermediate, or ultimate causes would exist. "Therefore it is necessary to admit a first efficient cause, to which everyone gives the name of God."[4] You cannot have effects without a cause, nor would the universe exist today without that primal cause.

The third and last of the cosmological arguments also owes its origin to Aristotelian distinctions. This time Aquinas utilizes the language of "possibility" versus "necessity." Sometimes philosophers prefer the language of "contingency" and "necessity." For Aquinas, the concept "possibility" carries with it the supposition that at some point a "contingent" entity will cease to be or non-exist. That means it had to be generated, became spent, and died. If everything's nature consists of "being," "becoming," and "not being," then "at one time there was nothing in existence," or so Aquinas concluded. At least, to his line of reasoning, it was theoretically likely that if everything were contingent, with only intermediate contingencies as pro-generators, which in turn decay and perish, then there could have been a time when nothing existed. And, if at one time nothing existed, then the universe would not exist today. Hence, there must exist of *necessity* an agent that is prior to the vast host of contingencies that have existed and exist now. Of necessity it has to be non-contingent, or an entity that has enjoyed and will always enjoy perpetual, necessary, and eternal existence, without beginning or end, namely God.

One value of Aquinas' third proof lies in its referent to the phenomenon of "nothing." If nothing existed prior to that which now exists, how could anything exist at all? How did the universe produce itself from nothing? Even theories of spontaneous creation (such as the Big Bang) require a pre-existing receptacle, space, and elementary matter, whether in the form of nano-particles, a potential electromagnetic field, or a Higgs boson—the long sought-after "God particle." Neither the ancient Sumerians, Plato, Aristotle, nor possibly even the Priestly writer of Genesis 1 presupposed

4. Ibid.

the "existence" of "nothing." Marduk, Zeus, the Demiurge, and YHWH all create out of a formless void, bringing order (*logos*), mind (*nous*), soul (*nephesh/psyche*), and life (*zoé*) to an otherwise chaotic sea of dark, pre-existent mass. It is only in 2 Maccabees 7:28 that the idea of a creation *ex nihilo*, out of nothing, appears for the first time in Jewish thought. By Aquinas' time, Christian philosophy had fully adopted the anti-Gnostic position that God's creation of the universe was entirely a product of God's beneficent will, resulting in the creation of "all things visible and invisible" (as affirmed in the Nicene Creed). Had God created out of anything pre- or co-existent with God, then God would not be the sole reality of the universe. This concern remains a viable issue for traditional Western theologians, if God did not create *ex nihilo*.

Few have assessed the cosmological argument with the perspicuity that Paul Tillich brought to the scene. For Tillich, the question of God has to be asked. It is unavoidable. Tillich notes that in the act of asking any question, an unconditional element is present. The God question must be asked "because the threat of nonbeing, which man experiences as anxiety, drives him to the question of being conquering nonbeing and of courage conquering anxiety."[5] In Tillich's mind, our finitude compels us to pose the question of God's existence. The whole categorical structure of finitude presses man to ask it. Where God is the answer, the courage for overcoming anxiety is assured. Tillich warns that the cosmological argument, along with the others, represents, at best, a cluster of "hypostatized" queries. As "proofs" they lose their power and appeal, because they lose their "categorical character." Being has to include courage, but being "cannot maintain courage against the ultimate threat of nonbeing" without "a basis for ultimate courage."[6] Thus, in Tillich's view, the value of the cosmological argument lies in its power to quell man's fear of nonbeing.

The historian of philosophy, Frederick Copleston, also weighed in with his assessment of the cosmological argument in his now-famous debate with Bertrand Russell in the 1940s.[7] For Copleston, all three of Aquinas' first ways are of lasting value, because they demonstrate that God's existence can be proven by metaphysical arguments. Furthermore, they affirm that without God's existence, man's moral and religious experiences would lose their foundational validity. Moreover, they establish the

---

5. Tillich, *Systematic*, Vol. 1, 208.

6. Ibid., 209

7. Copleston and Russell, "Third Programme of the British Broadcasting Corporation," 209.

fact that, if there were no necessary being (i.e., "no being which must exist and cannot not-exist") then "nothing would exist."[8] The necessity of God's existence remained of extreme importance to Copleston, as without it, no absolute standards could be postulated for guiding human existence. As he cherished repeating: "Without an Absolute Being, there can be no absolute values." Which is precisely Aquinas' fourth argument.

Aquinas labeled his "fourth way" as "taken from the graduation to be found in things": the good, true, noble, and the real, along with all other referents, require a "maximum" standard or "cause." Otherwise their presence or our awareness of them would make no sense. Since God is the "maximum," the Ground of Being, possessing all perfections befitting God, God must be the cause or standard of any kind of "being, goodness, and every other perfection" found in man.[9] However clear this might appear on paper, nonetheless, Aquinas' fourth way confused two issues. These he lumped together without distinction. The first and most apparent issue has to do with the *natures of things* in general, or objects and persons per se. All are different as particulars of the universal maximum which they mirror, a principle that he acknowledged he owed to Aristotle's *Metaphysics*. But acknowledging differences requires the *exercise of judgmen*t, or the capacity to draw distinctions based on whatever normative principle a person chooses to favor. Such judgments can be challenged if they cannot be justified, or if they are based solely on personal choice, emotions, or unexamined suppositions. For Aquinas, God is the only sufficient standard whose perfect nature contains the principles by means of which all moral and ethical distinctions can be based, as well as all ontological and structural differences be distinguished. What is absent in all this, however, is any recognition of "perspectivism," a concept which the ancient Sophists favored, but which Plato and Aristotle rejected. The latter did so because it undermined their quests for that beyond which no higher standard exists. A major part of their flaw lay in their metaphysics and their limited understanding of how nature's biophysical concurrences operate. From whose perspective do you make a *judgment* concerning *content*? That is the Catch-22. For Aquinas, God is both the criterion for making any *judgment* as well as the standard governing *gradations* of being.

It fell to Immanuel Kant to shift the focus of the moral argument, which led him to espouse a category of "practical reason" to establish the

---

8. Ibid., 243

9. Aquinas, cited in Hick, *Classical and Contemporary Readings*, 42.

existence of God. It grew out of his distinction between the phenomenal and *noumenal* worlds which scientists and philosophers examine. The phenomenal world of appearance is the domain science studies. It achieves this by bringing the categories of reason to bear on sense perception and its objects—things out there. Moral philosophy, however, has to do with the *noumenal* world of "things-in-themselves," such as human beings whose wills are not governed by the limits of cause and effect. For morality to have meaning at all, the human will must enjoy both freedom of choice and hope of fulfillment. To guarantee the reality of the highest principle of choice as well as protect and advance life's *summum bonum*, a Reality must exist who embodies the highest of all principles as well as guarantees a future in which the choice of good is rewarded. Hence, God—the only Reality who can fulfill the above—must exist and provide immortality as the reward for man's effort.[10] In this light, Copleston's insistence on the existence of an Absolute Being as the foundation for Absolute values is a principle drawn primarily from Kant.

Finally, Aquinas' fifth way is known as an argument from design or contrivance. He describes it as "taken from the governance of the world." It is also known as a teleological argument, inasmuch as it posits the belief that everything drives toward an end (its *telos*), for which it has been designed. Natural bodies have been designed to act the way they do, insofar as they are incapable of choosing this end for themselves. "Whatever lacks knowledge cannot move toward an end, unless it be directed by some being endowed with knowledge and intelligence . . . and this being we call God."[11] Of all Aquinas' arguments, that from design—an argument from effects to cause—is deemed his least satisfactory today. Our knowledge of the Big Bang and Evolution undercuts any need to posit an intelligent Designer to account for how either nature or human beings came into existence or behave the way they do. Still the teleological argument is not without merit. The sheer beauty of the universe, the awe it inspires, as well as the quest for purpose it encourages mankind to seek, bolsters its usefulness as an element of the human condition one cannot escape. It too, according to Tillich, owes its appeal to human finitude and man's fear of meaninglessness unless a higher purpose exists in which man's anxiety can be assuaged.

---

10. See Kant's *The Metaphysical Foundation of Morals* along with his *Critique of Practical Reason*.

11. Hick, *Classical and Contemporary Readings*, 42.

CHAPTER 6

Science and the Universe

According to astrophysicists, our universe burst into existence some 13.8 billion years ago. Imagine a night of infinite darkness suddenly illuminated by a stupendous fireball. Hot light, silhouetted against a screen of infinitesimal particles, violently bursts into flame. Cores of glowing sub-atomic quarks hurtle wildly into space. The brilliant glow increases in size, spewing its treasure of glistening energy in every direction. Waves of radiation race toward the farthest ends of the night. Bands of purple, indigo, pink, and gold drift amid the twinkling wonder as gravity is born, spinning off shimmering galactic masses of gas and future stars. Within minutes, electrons, protons, and neutrons appear; then the heavier atoms of carbon, iron, potassium, uranium, and oxygen take form.

In time, interstellar debris collects to form a universe of myriad stars, including our own galaxy and, ultimately, our planet Earth. Billions of more years creep across time before our sun can penetrate the gases that hover over its surface, but slowly the clouds open, vapors enwrap the orbiting bulge, temperatures cool, rains swell its volcanic cavities, and levels of oxygen rise to sustain the first amebic colonies. For another billion years, great swaths of algae and simpler life forms struggle to take hold, until amphibians, plants, and higher life forms evolve to herald the coming of an as-yet unimagined species, namely our own.

Modern science traces our human origins from a minimum of 1–2 million years ago to a maximum of 3–4. According to anthropologists, humanity "descended" from a line of hominids whose ancestors in turn are traceable to hominoids who inhabited treetops thirty million years ago.

SCIENCE AND THE UNIVERSE

Somewhere between the Oligocene and Miocene Epics, hominoids branched into two main divisions: pongids, or apes, and hominids who became the ancestors of humankind. By the mid Miocene Epic (26 million years ago), hominoids had already developed upright postures, mastered hand-over-hand travel, along with lengthened limbs, versatile arm and hip sockets, broad chests, and strong collar bones. As the zoologist Paul Weisz has dubbed them, they had become veritable "tree-walkers." With amazing agility, they began to explore their endless arboreal realm. As their brain size increased, so did their sensory powers. Their ability to see, clutch, and roam the canopied domain that fed and sheltered them quickened their curiosity and enhanced their self-awareness. Communication patterns and social contact evolved, along with stronger bodies and more adept thumbs for fleeing snakes and grasping newborn.[1]

At some juncture in the mid-to-late Tertiary Period (eleven million years ago), hominids abandoned their arboreal canopy and "descended" to the ground. This change to a new environment required faster and more mobile bodies; it increased socialization for protection and led to an early use of primitive tools. By three million years ago in Africa, the savanna-roaming Australopithecus and later Homo habilis emerged, paving the way for the future of mankind. It seems now certain that about one million years ago, Homo erectus entered the scene, a true bi-pedal, pre-historic man. Soon thereafter, Neanderthal and, finally, Homo sapiens made their way into Northern European and Asian climes. At last the stage was set for modern humankind to begin its continuing quest and intellectual adventure of "transcendence." As Weisz surmises: Thus, man "is able to think in a new time dimension . . . the future; . . . He is able to plan, to reason out the consequences of future actions, . . . to choose by deliberation, and to have aims and purposes, . . . to think in symbolic terms, . . . to envision beauty and to weep and to laugh."[2] Behold, humankind, with our capacity for transcendence, had arrived. And, with our arrival, the quest and hunger for our Ground of Being began, along with our fears and veneration of that inescapable Self we came to call, "God."

This astounding story, if anything, should underwrite the possibility of a Ground of Being at least as magnificent as the universe itself. Leading scientists, however, decline to embrace such an option. In particular, both

---

1. See Paul Weisz, *Science of Zoology*, opening chapters, as well as Stephen Hawking's *A Brief History of Time*.

2. Weisz, *Science of Zoology*, 428–30.

45

Stephen Hawking and Edward Wilson—one a physicist, the other a biologist—reject the need for any artificer to have begun the process of creation. For Hawking, the Big Bang was spontaneous. In his mind, given the laws of nature, namely, the electromagnetic principles of physics, no divine guidance or presence is detectable or required to explain the emergence of the universe. On its own, it expanded and colonized the night with billions upon billions of glowing galactic stars.[3]

In particular, Hawking asks: "Why is there something rather than nothing?" Second, "Why do we exist?" And third: "Why this particular set of laws and not some others?" To arrive at a sufficient answer to each, he postulates what he calls the "M-theory." M-theory stands for "model-dependent realism," which is "based on the idea that our brains interpret the input from our sensory organs by making a model of the universe."[4] (Kant, anyone?) Once such a model is conceptualized, it enables us to account for the events that comprise the universe. However, to be acceptable to science, all such models must "accurately predict the same events." In fact, M-theory allows for the possibility of numerous universes, each of which would be the direct derivative of physical laws. Claims Hawking:

> According to M-theory, ours is not the only universe. Instead, M-theory predicts that a great many universes were created out of nothing. Their creation does not require the intervention of some supernatural being or god. Rather . . . they arise naturally from physical law.[5]

After providing a series of chapters in support of quantum physics (an explanation of particles, waves, and quarks), Hawking answers the three questions above. "The universe is comprehensible because it is governed by scientific laws."[6] These in turn arose from the Big Bang. They are: gravity, electromagnetism, and the two nuclear forces of radioactivity and the force that holds protons and neutrons together. They are the result of the Big Bang. Finally, after further discussion, Hawking concludes:

> Because there is a law like gravity, the universe can and will create itself from nothing. . . . Spontaneous creation is the reason there is something rather than nothing, why the universe exists, why

---

3. Hawking, *Grand Design*, 10.
4. Ibid., 7.
5. Ibid., 7–8.
6. Ibid., 87.

we exist. It is not necessary to invoke God to light the blue touch paper and set the universe going.[7]

Hawking's *The Grand Design* may not please religious persons committed to God the Creator, or even to Plato's God without a "beginning," or Anselm's "that than which none greater can be conceived." Nonetheless, Hawking's insistence on spontaneous creation—given the laws of nature and that densely packed black hole of matter that exploded—allows for a conscientious concept of God to emerge, one that is free of doctrines based on the methodology of philosophical determinism and "intellectual ascent." From this perspective, it is possible to view God as the Ground of that intense spark, of that stupendous Bang, that required only time and chance to create the world as we know it. To do so obviates the need to invent an artificer that neither observation nor science can postulate as necessary for that cosmic miracle of 13 billion years ago. In this light, Whitehead and Hartshorne's convictions about God appear closer to the truth than religious myths and dogmatic pronouncements.

If Hawking's assessment of the universe's origin obviates religion's need for a Creator, then Edward Wilson's *The Social Conquest of Earth* completes God's dismissal as a requirement for the emergence of Homo sapiens. In a manner similar to Hawking's, Wilson raises three questions of his own. Asks Wilson: "Where do we come from? What are we? Where are we going?" In brief, he answers that we are biological creatures, who have evolved over a long period of time, and, thanks to our capacity of socialization, have managed to survive and perpetuate ourselves around the earth. In all of this, no divine intervention or guidance has ever occurred, nor is it needed to explain our rise as human beings. Writes Wilson:

> Humanity is a biological species in a biological world. . . . Although exalted in many ways, we remain an animal species of the global fauna. Our lives are restrained by the two laws of biology: all of life's entities and processes are obedient to the laws of physics and chemistry: and all of life's entities and processes have arisen through evolution by natural selection.[8]

Wilson fears that the more people rely on creation myths and belief in God, the greater harm they bring to themselves and others. Only a spirit of cooperation among intelligent and enlightened persons, committed to

---

7. Ibid., 180.
8. Wilson, *Social Concept of Earth*, 286.

a love of science, its methods, truth, and findings, can guarantee our personal, group, and planet's survival. Science is not just an interesting discipline or alternative view of life among many. It is the "wellspring" of all our knowledge. It is not religion's "coequal," nor do religious views constitute a coequal equivalent. The conflict between the two is "irreconcilable." A chasm exists that can only bring "no end of trouble as long as religious leaders go on, making unsupportable claims about supernatural causes of reality."[9]

One may not care for Wilson's views, nor his opposition to organized religion, but the truth of our emergence as a biological species over a long period of time, with an equally long and varied history of development—both culturally and intellectually—is beyond refutation. If God exists or God's existence matters, then the reality of the universe as it is and our knowledge of our species' evolution requires a knowledge of God compatible with this truth. That is why God as the Ground of Being, or our inescapable ability to evade the phenomenon of the "depths," provides both a philosophical and phenomenological counterweight to atheism. Even the spontaneous explosion of the universe's dark matter requires a cause, along with the phenomenological capacity of self-transcendence. Although neither Hawking nor Wilson approve of, nor foresee, any need for continued belief in God, the yearnings of mankind have found sincere fulfillment in the universal cry so poignantly uttered by Israel's enduring psalmist:

> When I consider thy heavens, the work of thy fingers, the moon and the stars, which thou hast ordained; What is man, that thou art mindful of him? And the son of man, that thou visitest him? (Ps 8:3–4, AV)

Wilson is right to reject those organized religions whose taboos and tenets perpetuate irrelevant doctrines that no longer speak to humanity today, but his declaration that God is unnecessary to the universe falls short of mankind's longing for that self-understanding that only transcendence can satisfy. Where God is understood as the answer to humanity's depths, then all tension between science and religion fades away.

This is strangely corroborated by science itself. Though always an embarrassment to scientists, even its own members occasionally experience paranormal activity beyond their discipline's capacity to explain. When a neurosurgeon in 2008 experienced an out-of-body journey, he was shocked

---

9. Ibid., 295.

to acknowledge how real it was. Falling into a coma in which that part of his brain's cortex that controls thought and feelings had shut down, nevertheless, he realized his "conscious, inner self was alive and well." As Dr. Alexander describes it: "While the neurons of my cortex were stunned to complete inactivity . . . , my brain-free consciousness journeyed to another, larger dimension of the universe." He found himself in a place of "big, puffy, pink-white" clouds, set off against the "blue-black sky." Above the clouds, "flocks of transparent, shimmering beings arched across the sky." The silvery bodies made a beautiful sound, and an angelic presence reassured him that he was loved, had nothing to fear, and could do no wrong. When he awoke from his coma, he realized he had experienced *spiritually* the truth that modern physics hails: that our universe is truly a unity, that all of it is woven together, that no true separation exists. Even more so, Alexander was now joyfully compelled to acknowledge that the universe is equally defined by "love."[10]

It is likely that science will one day discover a neurological explanation for such experiences. Perhaps the mind holds fast briefly to a dream that snatches the consciousness up into its esoteric domain before our consciousness flickers out and the last molecules of oxygen are used up. In that brief, intense moment, our happiest and surest fantasies rush forward to guard our dreamlike sleep. Upon awakening, we remember that intense joy and bliss that lovingly overshadowed our slumbering unconsciousness. Yet, in rebuff of our own mind's struggle to explain the phenomenon, why shouldn't the creative energy that pulsates out from the Ground of Being manifest itself in us as a shimmering transparent light, an inexorable calm that bears us up into its supreme Bliss? It is certainly worth pondering. If anything, this whole phenomenon should dispel any notion that consciousness is devoid of either metaphysical or spiritual repositories that enrich our sense of personhood. They enjoy an actuality, if not equal to, at least compatible with our physiological structure. One might dare to say that they qualify as components of our cellular structure, as defined by quantum physics.

There is a spiritual nuance about the earth, about mankind's affinity with the physical universe, that is undeniable. Every religion values it. We see it in Buddhism's reverence for snow-capped mountains and their icy winds that stir Tibetan prayer flags, or spin old whirling prayer wheels. It appears again in Taoism's submission to the Way and its Power, as well as in

---

10. See Eben Alexander, *Newsweek*, October 15, 2012, 30–32.

Christianity and Jesus' love of nature. "Behold, the lilies of the field. . . . Not even Solomon in all his glory was arrayed as one of these" (Matt 6:28–29).

J. S. Baxter once captured a glimpse of this in his picturesque allusion to God as: "He who paints the wayside flower as well as lights the evening star."[11] The spirituality of the earth speaks to us in every season. The cycles of time and the stages of life reflect each other as well as nurture and sustain the soul. Our self-identity is inseparable from the ebb and tide of the oceans, from the circular splendor of the moon and stars, as well as the savage grandeur of Earth's fauna and flora. All about us, the universe sings its song of glory, resplendent with magic, mystery, terror, and wonder.

---

11. See Al Bryant, *Climbing the Heights*, 340.

CHAPTER 7

The Voice of Being Speaks Many Languages

SPIRITUALITY IS GLOBAL. SINCE humankind stood erect, became mobile, and left behind majestic handprints on cave walls, their sense of belonging to life's larger cycles has defined humankind's ascent. In time, every culture has adopted some form of religious self-identification. Whether matriarchal, esoteric, exotic, or patriarchal; dogmatic, magisterial, erotic, or otherworldly; contemporary, enlightened, open-minded, or ecstatic, the Voice of Being has found a home in humanity's continual quest for meaning. To narrow the choices to one, or to insist that the Voice of Being speaks only one language, violates everything we know about our evolution, our multiple languages, along with our cultural and spiritual heritages.

This is as true of individual holy men and women, as it is of institutions and groups. The monastic life is as universal as Wilson's tribal organizations. The monks and nuns of Christianity, the sadhus of Hinduism, the arahants and nuns of Buddhism, the mystics of Islam, as well as the masters of Zen all mirror the depths of Being in their respective time and place. Each has much to learn from the other. None carries the totality of life's nectar in his or her burnished cup. A monk's humility, self-sacrifice, and love echo Being's quiet pulse as much as the trumpet's note and angelic voices of institutional choirs herald the same.

The religions of India provide an extraordinary window onto the world's openness to Being. Behind all of the multiple forms of Hindu ritual, meditation, and belief stands a core of religious principles that unites the many voices into a harmonious witness of Being. Of foremost importance is the conviction that all are part of a larger reality, spiritually known as God, and metaphysically known as Brahman. The central goal of life is to become aware of one's true essence as a manifestation of God. Strong egos oppose this reality and require many rebirths until the realization is achieved. Christianity may be hesitant to state as much, but as the Swami Paramahansa Yogananda has explained: "By banishing ego-consciousness, man awakens to his divine identity, his oneness with the sole Life, God."[1] What Christianity's Reformed Tradition rejects is any blurring of the separation between God, the Creator, and man, his creation. This "infinite qualitative distinction" must not be lost, nor is it, in a sense, for the Swami.

Yogananda's concept of God's immanence is not unlike Hartshorne's. For both we are a microcosm of the transcendence and immanence of God in all things—from the mystery of the atom to the inescapability of God-consciousness in human beings. That at death we do not unbecome but become part of the memory and will of God is a tenet in both Process theology and Brahmanic thought. It is as central to spirituality as the quantum theory is to understanding the universe. We are living sparks of the Big Bang and carry in our genetic code and subconscious framework the wondrous evolution of millions of years. Creation is still unfolding in each of us. Christianity may not accept reincarnation, but its doctrine of the resurrection envisions a future opportunity to continue evolving with the universe and its Creator. In that regard, it mirrors aspects of Hinduism's doctrine of reincarnation. Why should we not be part of a shimmering quantum world that the neurosurgeon Alexander experienced?

Equally important in Hindu thought is the concept "karma." The realization that our choices and actions today have been shaped by our choices and actions of yesterday and in turn will shape our choices and actions tomorrow is compatible with any universal theory of cause and effect. Critics of karma who label it "fatalism" fail to realize that the survival of the wisest has always incorporated self-accountability. Existentialist thought, which tends to deny any form of essentialism, has structured its house of hope on a similar requirement, acknowledging the need of each person to shape his or her own history. For existentialists, if we are to have any authentic life, it must be one that we choose, however limited our circumstances may be. The voice of Being is equally heard in Einstein's theory of relativity. The where, when, and chemical makeup of anything in space and time—given

---

1. Yogananda, *Sayings of Paramahansa Yogananda*, 114.

the dynamics of electromagnetism, gravity, and radio-activity—shape the essential character of the phenomenal world in which we live. We are a sparkling pulsation of all this. Christianity may reject any notion of our being a physical or intellectual extension of God; nonetheless, God's immanence as a noetic factor of our self-consciousness is undeniable.

A third critical insight in Hinduism is the phenomenon "maya." Often defined as "illusion," maya is the differentiated world of separate entities and egos. In truth, all such fragments of being are nothing other than Brahman, manifestations of the sole reality, God. As Yogananda explains: "The whole universe is made of Spirit. . . . A star, a stone, a tree, and a man are equally composed of the Sole Substance, God." In order to create a diversified universe, God "had to impose on everything the *appearance* of individuality."[2] Lest one assume that maya violates the Second and Third Judeo-Christian Commandments, Yogananda infers that the Commandments only imply "that we should not exalt the objects of creation above the Creator."[3] Love for the things of nature or family are never meant to displace "the supreme throne in our hearts," occupied by God alone, he asserts. Once we realize this, we are free from the veils of delusion and become one with God. To be able to find God in one another is one of life's treasured goals. If nothing else, maya operates as a religious metaphor for the interrelationship of all things. It may not be provable in cognitive or representative form; nonetheless, the insight captures what science proclaims in its own theorems. What religion adds is the salt of reverence and the fullest measure of awe and joy.

Theravada Buddhism constitutes yet another language with respect to the Voice of Being. It too knows of the veils of illusion in its quest for true enlightenment. As in the case of Hinduism, until the craving self is extinguished, there can be no peace with the self, or the THATNESS of the universe. In many ways, it is less esoteric and more scientific than Hinduism. To become one with the essence of all things, to recognize one's interrelatedness with the phenomena that pervade all things, and to acknowledge one's impermanence, brings harmony and peace.

Its Four Noble Truths are also in keeping with the dynamic evolution of the universe: 1) suffering is universal; as evolution is not without struggle, conflict, and change. 2) Much of this struggle is rooted in craving, in the mix and warp of atoms, cells, species, and cultures vying with each other in an attempt to achieve fulfillment. It is an inescapable facet of life. 3)

2. Ibid., 10.
3. Ibid., 48–49.

Only the cessation of craving and the extinction of a selfish ego can eliminate universal suffering. As long as each entity strives to accumulate more and more, leaving less and less for others, the exponential consequence for increased suffering rises daily; and 4), this can only be stopped by choosing the Middle Path—the way that avoids mindless austerities on the one hand and unrestrained indulgence on the other. One can argue that Theravada Buddhism is mistaken to think it can "escape" evolution's inevitable ruptures, changes, and growing pains. Yet, its "craving" for peace with the THATNESS of the universe constitutes one of its noblest appeals. To accept the universe as it is, to acknowledge one's finite, or impermanent and mortal nature, and to cease questing for that which cannot be supported by science or reason is commendable. Theravada's response to the Voice of Being represents a mature call to conform to the limits of what is best for all. It challenges one to wake up and become enlightened as the Buddha did; and, when one dies, to die with dignity, knowing that only two things survive—one's attitude and the karmic activities for good or evil that one's life has set in motion. It is a sobering voice, spoken in the language of compassion, and often with suffering, renunciation, and patience. The Buddha may not have died on a cross, but in his time and culture he represented an incarnation of life's higher vision.

The Dalai Lama has also raised his voice in both English and in the language of his Tibetan inheritance. As he has stated so humbly: "I myself am just a human being, and incidentally a Tibetan, who chooses to be a Buddhist monk."[4] In keeping with his Buddhist past, he endorses the "fundamental precept of . . . Interdependence," which he links with karma.[5] Specifically, it is motivation and action that define the human experience. For the Dalai Lama, "a being's consciousness contains an imprint of all . . . past experiences and impressions, and the actions which preceded them. That is known as *karma*."[6] It is a facet as important as *impermanence* and *interdependence*. Where such principles are accepted, the sanctity of life and the desire for truth, justice, and understanding have a chance to triumph over ignorance and despair.[7]

The Dalai Lama takes pride in fostering inter-faith dialogue. He considers it an aspect of "Universal Responsibility." He defines the latter as "the

---

4. Dalai Lama, *Freedom in Exile*, xiii.
5. Ibid., 10.
6. Ibid.
7. Ibid., 81.

responsibility we all have for each other and for all sentient beings and also for all of Nature."[8] He disfavors the establishment of a "super religion" that would eclipse the unique voice of each. Because each person's spiritual needs are different, "different spiritual medicines are required."[9] In the final analysis, "all religions aim at making people better" and at helping them find happiness.

It is doubtful that either Hawking or Wilson would disagree with His Holiness' conclusion.

Perhaps few ears have ever been as close to the Voice of Being as the Sioux Holy Man Black Elk. His understanding of the four quadrants of nature, or the cycles of life represented by the cardinal directions of East, South, West, and North, is unsurpassable. To these Great Grandfathers, plus Father Sky and Mother Earth, he draws upon the traditions of his elders to win his Lakota Peoples' allegiance to the nurturing qualities of the Plains Indian's life: wisdom, compassion, courage, and reverence. Behind it all, stands One Great Spirit, Creator and Giver of life. Few parables are as touching as his rendition of the Buffalo Calf Woman. In her gift of herself to the Sioux Nation, she clothes, feeds, shelters, and strengthens them for life's fourfold cycle: birth, youth, adulthood, and old age. All of it is symbolized in Black Elk's reverence for nature and the cosmic order behind it.[10] That well-intentioned Christian missionaries tried to drown out his eloquent voice witnesses to the shame of all authoritative approaches of religion. In the end, they violate the spirit of their own founders as well as throttle the quiet voice of Being. Even Jesus loved nature and drew lessons from it. Figs, grapevines, thistles and weeds; poppies, wind, waves, and sea all witness to the Father's grandeur, providence, and care for all.

Nor is Zen or Taoism to be disparaged. Quiet and personal, each supports an individual's quest for peace and harmony, balance and stability, within the self, as well as with the universe.

Take Taoism. Its founder, Lao-Tzu, is as enigmatic today as he was in his time (b. 604 BCE). According to legend, he was a native of the state of Ch'u. Although born in a tiny hamlet, in time he became a scholar, historian, and archivist for the province of Chou. Legend claims that upon his retirement, he was halted at the city's gates and asked to provide a book of wisdom. The request resulted in *The Tao Te Ching*. Scholars doubt the veracity of such a story, but somewhere within Lao-Tzu's timeframe (551–450 BCE), the collection of enigmatic sayings came into being. How many are his, or someone else's, we

---

8. Ibid., 200.
9. Ibid.
10. See Neihardt, *Black Elk Speaks*, 5f.

may never know. Nonetheless, the philosophy of *The Way and Its Power* has tantalized readers and followers alike for years.

The impressive distinction about Taoism lies in its pure naturalism. No gods or meditative agenda, rituals, or rules are requisite for Taoism to work its calming powers. Nor are any dogmatic, magisterial, or arcane beliefs imposed on a Taoist. To accept the flow of the universe, to bring one's life in harmony with its calm or turbulent cycles, and to live in peace with oneself and others constitute its principal goals. Religion historian Huston Smith quite ably summarizes the movement's tenets.

First, *the Tao is the way of ultimate reality*.[11] It lies just beyond our perception, underneath our powers to penetrate life's fullest secrets. In that regard, it shares something metaphysically with Tillich's Ground of Being. It transcends our concepts and ideas; is both ineffable and transcendent. Like Brahman, it pervades all things but escapes linguistic capture.

> The way that can be spoken of
> Is not the constant way;
> The name that can be named
> Is not the constant name.[12]

Anything that can be said of the Way can never be true or false. There is no language adequate to explain it. Even the word "tao" is at best a metaphor, a substitute for the all-pervasive, inexplicable, and incomprehensible Mystery that grounds all existence. Not even the Big Bang as a theory can penetrate beyond the BANG itself. Other than explaining the origin of the universe, the Big Bang cannot offer a single reason for, or even the purpose of, the universe. It's just here, now, changing and flowing like a river emptying into the sea. Indeed, why are we even driven to want to impose a concept on that which sustains and underlies the universe? "I am who I am," said God. "That is sufficient for you," he told Moses. "Why do you need to know anything more?" We don't, answer Taoists.

Second, according to Smith, *the Tao is the way of the universe*.[13] If the first principle captures its transcendent nature, the second adumbrates its immanent feature. The Tao is immanent, the ever-present organizing principle. Like John's *logos* in the Gospel of John, not only in the beginning was Tao, but without Tao was not anything made that was made. In Tao

---

11. Huston Smith, *World's Religions*, 198.
12. See Lao Tzu, *Tao Te Ching*, 57.
13. Ibid., 198.

THE VOICE OF BEING SPEAKS MANY LANGUAGES

is life and light. It encapsulates the Way of life. The Taoist term, explains Smith, is "wu-wei," symbolized by water, with an emphasis on surrender and submission,

> Highest good is like water. Because water excels in benefiting myriad creatures without contending with them and settles where none would like to be, it comes close to the way.[14]

In this regard, the Tao is subtle, taking the path of least resistance, yet powerful enough to sweep away stubborn objects in its path. In the end, Tao prevails, for in time it wears down the hardest stone. Wu-wei is the ultimate power. It is often symbolized in Zen Gardens as weathered, sunken stones, barely visible beneath a garden's sea of raked pebbles.

Third, Tao offers itself as *the ordering principle by which mankind should live.*[15] It constitutes a practical moral and personal ethic by which to engage in life's affairs. People who follow it are more likely to survive than those who resist. Do not take on more than you can shoulder. Do not fight the inevitable. Do not contend against that which is not in your power. In this respect, it shares something in the way of Epictetus' Stoic philosophy. Change what you can but accept what you can't. It is an engaging way of life and belief. Above all, it is compatible with our scientific knowledge of the universe and Darwinism.

Many of its contemporary adherents often establish colonies of likeminded souls, who withdraw from society and seek solace and quietude in forest places and mountain enclaves. There, close to nature, by a flowing stream, protruding rock, and wind and rain, one quietly passes one's life in accordance with nature. That the Voice of Being should whisper its wisdom in the call to solitude is as commendable as the mendicant way of Hindu, Buddhist, and Christian monks and nuns.

Zen is but another step, equally direct, discrete, and attune to that silent Enlightenment that frees one vis-à-vis the self and the universe. Few have interpreted its fascinating vision as engagingly as D. T. Suzuki. His many books aptly explain Zen's significance for the modern era. As Suzuki maintains, Zen "is one of the most important aspects of Buddhism, claiming to transmit the essence and spirit of Buddhism directly."[16] For Zen, "personal experience . . . is everything." Without such direct experi-

---

14. Ibid., 64.
15. Smith, *World Religions*, 189.
16. Suzuki, *Zen Buddhism*, 32.

ence, nothing can be efficiently grasped. There exists no equivalence for the power of simple and unsophisticated experience. Concepts can never substitute for it. For that reason, Zen is not a philosophy. It sanctions no sacred texts, nor champions any sacred doctrines, nor obsesses over any soul to be saved. If asked, "What does Zen teach?" Suzuki replies: "Nothing." Whatever teachings may exist come out of one's own experience. "We teach ourselves; Zen merely points the way."[17] Its goal is to make the mind its own master. "Getting into the nature of one's mind is its fundamental objective."[18] Zen uses meditation, but meditation is not Zen. There are no objects or thoughts upon which one has to fix one's mind, no God, no higher concept of love, truth, or goodness, or even the Buddhist doctrine of impermanence. Such would confine or block the mind's openness to itself and the world. There are no obligatory objects of meditation. Zen's goal is not abstraction but perception and feeling. "The central fact of life as it is lived is what Zen aims to grasp."[19] It deals with the living facts of life. The truth of Zen is within everyone, where one must look for it oneself. This truth is practical and commonplace. Once attained, a person's eyes are opened to the greatest of mysteries, as life is daily and hourly performed.[20] Indeed, the "truth and power of Zen consists in its very simplicity, directness, and utmost practicalness."[21] For this reason, "Zen never explains, but only affirms. Life is fact and no explanation is necessary or pertinent. . . . To live—is that not enough?"[22]

There is comfort in Zen's quiet and unobtrusive, yet intense way of perceiving the self and the universe. Its obedience to the voice of being that it "feels" in itself requires no outward authoritative power to justify one's discovery of Enlightenment. If Zen possesses any "sacramental trappings" at all, they are found foremost in its Tea Ceremony, or highly symbolized pebble-raked Gardens, or in its aloof and mystic artworks and flowers. In all forms, one is drawn back to nature in its simplistic, rustic, and fundamental essence. In each there is no need to impose words, concepts, or search for some overwhelming question or purpose. To see, to feel, to accept what is

17. Ibid., 38.
18. Ibid., 70.
19. Ibid., 44.
20. Ibid., 45.
21. Ibid., 85.
22. Ibid., 71.

given, and give in return (as in the Tea Ceremony), is sufficient for living life as it is.

Western religions, with their emphasis on God, God's will, and humankind's purpose may be uncomfortable with Zen's quiescent submission to "what is." Nonetheless, it enjoys a compatibility with what we know to be true about the origin of the universe and humankind's climb to ascendancy. Having said this, however, Suzuki reminds his readers that Zen is *a mystical movement*, as well as *an intellectual and meditative one*. In his mind, life requires a mystic's approach to "what is." Why? Because Zen must never be confused with naturalism or libertinism—his quiet objection to Taoism per se—neither of which questions the value of life. Zen requires each of us to do that; otherwise, we are no different from animals, "which are lacking in moral intuition and religious consciousness."[23]

All of which brings us to the penultimate question: to what extent is God beyond good and evil?

---

23. Ibid., 86.

CHAPTER 8

Beyond Good and Evil

As suggested in chapter 1, any critical review of the question of God cannot avoid the issue of good and evil. God is beyond good and evil, inasmuch as good and evil are concepts that we have created in order to assess our human experiences and assign them value. One might perhaps clarify this claim by stating that God is "above" good and evil, yet that God is "good" in both an analogical and ontological way, which we experience and which reason dictates. Something of this phenomenological sense may well be mirrored in the ancient story of Jacob's dream of God's angels, "ascending and descending" the ladder, concerning which "the LORD" stood above it" (Gen 28:12–13). But we must not simply equate divine goodness and human goodness, for the latter is shaped by human cultures. Every culture and religion has generated some scale of criteria by means of which actions and consequences, desires and thoughts, can be considered helpful or harmful. Since the time of the Gilgamesh Epic and Hammurabi's Code (as echoed in the book of Exodus), human behavior has been judged good or bad, right or wrong, based on someone or some group's understanding of what advances or obstructs the greatest benefit of all. From a religious perspective, the Ten Commandments, the Hebrew Bible, the Code of Manu, the *Dhammapada*, the *Analects of Confucius*, *The Tao Te Ching*, the New Testament, and the Quran have each contributed to this quest of values.

From a secular viewpoint, the West has long agonized over theories of fairness and equity. This is true from the time of the *Code of Hammurabi*, Plato's *Republic*, Augustine's *The City of God*, the Justinian Code, along with the *Magna Carta,* and down through the philosophical works of numerous philosophers. Many of the latter have incorporated Judeo-Christian values, although today's theorists argue along more utilitarian lines.

The point, however, is that all such works—religious or secular—are the product of human thought, human hope, and human desire for value and order. To claim that any of these can be traced to God directly, or reveal, reflect, or channel the will of God is another matter. Such a claim can only be done within the bounds of one's respective philosophical or religious tradition. All such values are derivatives of our own experiences and yearning for justice, liberty, and happiness. Moreover, this quest occurs in a world where human societies compete, struggle, and survive vis-à-vis each other. In addition, it takes place in a world characterized by ever-changing planetary developments and natural events, such as the Earth's orbiting the sun from 93,000,000 miles out. All of this takes place while the planet is undergoing recurring cycles of ice and thaw, heat and cold, floods and volcanic activity, and the shifting of tectonic plates, the sum of which adds to the uncalculated fate of its global families.

Unfortunately, a distinction between *natural* and *ethical* evil has not always been honored. Natural disasters are one thing; moral problems another. In some instances, God is blamed for both. It is understandable, therefore, that the oft-repeated problem of evil is addressed anew in age after age. In general it takes the following form: "If God is good, then God would not allow chaos and discord to happen if he could do something about it; and if God is all-powerful, then God could do something about it. However, chaos and discord do occur. Therefore, we must conclude that God is either all-powerful but not all-good; that God is supremely good but not all-powerful; or that there is no God." People continue to ask: "Is God good or not? Is God all-powerful or not? Why won't God step in and stop evil? Why won't God make this a better world? Why do bad things have to happen to so many people, especially to little children and the poor? Why?"

Across the years, theologians have fashioned theodicies to resolve the problem, often favoring *the necessity of God allowing us the freedom required for moral choice* to address the dilemma. Without moral choice, it is argued, humans would be less than human. But for innocent children and the world's wretched to have to pay so high a price of suffering for such a noble reason begs an even larger question: who in the world would want to praise such a pitiless God or such a divine moral prig? Is it not wiser to search for a more reasonable cause for good and evil or one that avoids the logical dilemma above?

To posit that God is beyond good and evil merits scientific and philosophical consideration.

From a scientific viewpoint, the existence of the universe is a product of the Big Bang and of millions of years of evolution—even if sparked by Divine cause. It is the Big Bang that brought into being the atomic elements, the expansion of the universe, and the "laws" that govern "matter." Moreover, the emergence of the Solar System and the formation of our own planet, with all its eons of change and development, is the ingredient that has made life possible. Good and evil have nothing to do with this magnificent wonder. Instead, its very existence opens the way for ever-higher, more complex, and open-ended possibilities for its human population. We can make it "good" for ourselves, or "bad." And even when we fail, we can determine not to fail again. Good and evil belong to what we want for ourselves and others. The possibility for "good" is within everything and everyone. Every molecule, atom, quark, particle or electromagnetic wave; cell, organ, blood vessel, or synapse contains the possibility for the attainment of a unique "good." Particles that misfire are also part of the mix, endemic to the very nature of their atomic essence, whether in us or in things. The terms fortunate or unfortunate might apply, but not good or evil. The very nature of each thing contains within itself growth and development. Disasters will occur, random tragedies emerge; people will die. That is simply an aspect of the natural order. Whereas when bitter decisions in high places ignite bitter harvests, that is "bad," because human-caused human misery could have been averted. The Big Bang has made life possible in the natural and physical realm. Evolution has also shaped its form within. But it is we who make our lives good or bad, wonderful or evil, in the ethical realm.

In this regard, Hinduism, Buddhism, Taoism, and Zen possess a "leg up" on the West. Their metaphysical systems allow for and endorse conflict and disorder. In Hinduism, life and death, preservation and decay, are together manifestations of "what is," symbolized by the gods Vishnu and Shiva. The impersonal flow of existence is simply a condition of being itself. Neither good nor bad is assigned to this holistic reality. It is we who make it good or bad by our individual and collective karma, that is, by or our actions or inactions. Brahman, the Buddha-essence, the Taoist Way, or the Hindu gods are beyond good and evil. Each represents the sum total of all that encompasses and makes life possible. In the Eastern mind, to fault the nature of this reality reveals colossal ignorance, resulting in a life dominated by illusion and ego. To free oneself from such craving is the only answer and anodyne for universal suffering. Good and evil are inseparable from such suffering.

In our Western culture, it may also be argued that God is beyond good and evil because of God's *transcendent* nature. As Aquinas rightly reasoned, God exists analogically vis-à-vis man. The essence of God can only be grasped analogically, which means that God can only be defined in accordance with what is appropriate to God's nature, and man defined in accordance with what is true of his nature. What is true of us is neither univocally nor equivocally true of God. God stands apart, over against his creation. God enjoys an essence unique to God. While God is good and the highest good, God's goodness transcends our goodness.[1] God exists at a level totally unlike our own. In his fifth argument for the existence of God, as we have seen, Aquinas reasons that for any degree of perfection to have meaning, there must exist a perfect being who transcends all lesser perfections by means of whom the goodness and being of any creature is measured. His reasoning, however, belongs to the Platonic and Neoplatonic line that employs the methodology of intellectual ascent to establish the nature of God. It is purely a methodology of logical deduction, unbridled by the brutal, random, and raw facts of life. To ascribe the values of logical deduction, however, to the enigmatic powers prior to, or at work within, the Big Bang is problematic. Such a methodology belongs more to Randall's non-cognitive and non-representative view of the universe than to any cognitive or representative grasp of reality.

It is very possible that God's concerns for the universe have nothing to do with good or evil per se. Rather fulfillment, realization, and consciousness seem more in keeping with the true nature of the universe. Such developments in man can lead to gratitude, cooperation, serenity, thanksgiving and joy. In the final analysis, in both Christianity and Hinduism, a person's worth *is not measured* by his or her deeds of perfection. These will reap whatever good or bad karma they have set in motion. Rather *life is measured by the grandeur and grace of something higher*, whether called Brahman, forgiveness, or reincarnation. That puts God beyond good and evil, more creative and compelling than anything human measurements can devise. It brings peace to the saint or household laborer; to the Zen or Christian monk, whose life is open to the highest vistas of the soul's longings.

---

1. See Aquinas, *Summa Contra Gentiles*, 141–48.

Remember what Jesus said about God, who "makes his sun rise on the evil and on the good, and sends rain on the just and on the unjust" (Matt 5:45). It is reminiscent of Moses Maimonides' comment about Jacob's dream, during Jacob's flight to Haran. In his chapter fifteen of *The Guide for the Perplexed*, Maimonides reminds us that God stood "above" the ladder on which the angels were descending and ascending. God's position is unique, above and beyond even the reach of his angels (Gen 28:13).

If one were to ask the origin of good and evil, a host of resources would pop up. Philosophically, Being logically precedes non-Being, as non-Being is the opposite and antithesis of Being. If Being did not exist, non-Being would be nonsensical. To make non-Being prior would still require a something to make non-Being possible. Augustine appealed to this argument in his definition of evil as "the absence of good." Since God is perceived as the transcendent, uncaused causer of the universe, God's existence is ipso facto valued as a good. Plato used this argument in his *Timaeus*, as mentioned in chapter 2. Nonetheless, the Divine Causer still transcends our perceptions of good and evil, or being and non-being. "My ways are not your ways, nor my thoughts your thoughts." Or as Krishna was compelled to explain to Arjuna, "Intelligence . . . birth, death, fear, fearlessness . . . austerity, charity, fame and infamy are created by ME alone."[2] All of which in turn the Swami Prabhupada interprets as applicable to one's embodiment in the physical world.[3] Good and evil, right and wrong, harm or fortune, belong to this side of time. God is larger than all these antitheses and embraces the total framework of time and place, whether physical or spiritual. To accept life for its grateful opportunities, now and for all time, constitutes man's highest hope. God will take care of the rest. Just do your part, with wakefulness and gratitude, Krishna urges.

In Christianity, this transcendence is matched by John's classic text: "For God sent the Son into the world, not to condemn the world, but that the world might be saved through him" (John 3:17). It is grace, opportunity, possibility, and hope that define the mystery of the Uncaused Causer behind our consciences and consciousness. It is that Mystery that defines God more than good or evil. Otherwise we should never be satisfied with life, blaming a less than all-powerful and all-good God for the "evils" that befall us (natural or ethical), which constitute life's inevitable miseries.

2. See the Swami Prabhupada's translation of the *Bhagavad-Gita as It Is*, 164.
3. Ibid., 165.

Having postulated the above, however, does not account for evil itself. There may be no one universal explanation that resolves the issue definitively. Each culture and timeframe has had to wrestle with it independently. One contemporary thinker who has wrestled with the problem at length is Paul Ricoeur. His book *The Symbolism of Evil* is a masterpiece of philosophical and linguistic research. Biblical and Western myths constitute the focus of his investigation, but his analyses and conclusions shine with relevant insight. Before summarizing his views, however, his reference to the Orphic myths requires a brief glance at Hindu thought.

We do not know when the ideas of *soul* and *metempsychosis* (i.e., rebirth) first made their way into Greek thought. Plato certainly drew on both, thanks to the influence of the Orphic myths and the mystical philosophy of Pythagoras. Long before either of the latter became prevalent, however, Indian philosophers had already established the "reality" of soul and reincarnation. Its history is long and complicated but capably adumbrated by Yogi Ramacharaka in his *The Philosophies and Religions of India*.

Ramacharaka characterizes India's earliest philosophical years as falling into three periods: 1) the philosophy of the first sages, 2) Kapila's Sankhya System, and 3) the later Vedanta System. In the first stage the concept THAT prevailed. THAT represented the underlying mystery and totality of the universe. As such, the phenomenal world retained no abiding, constant, fixed, or imperishable qualities. Underlying this changing world of senses, however, something REAL and SUBSTANTIAL had to exist to account for the phenomenal world. It had to be ONE in reality to account for the world's unity, as well as transcend the world's attributes. Equally, it had to be ETERNAL and the UNCAUSED CAUSER of all else, or something would have existed prior to it. Nor could it change, as there was nothing else it could have been or could be, thus this ONE REALITY—THAT—has always existed and "as THAT . . . must be ALL that IS."[4] Inexpressible in words alone, yet amenable to reason, it contains its own LAW, however abstract and difficult to surmise. It is only in understanding this TRUTH that one is liberated from the recurring cycles of THAT and emancipated from its chain of existences. In Ramacharaka's mind, all the great sages up to and including the Buddha accepted the reality of THAT.

It was only with the coming of Kapila (around 700 BCE) that a second period arose. During this period, Kapila returned India to a more

---

4. See Ramacharaka, *Philosophies and Religions of India*, 35.

ancient time, known as "Sankhya," which means "perfect classification."[5] The Sankhya system maintained that two active principles alone interacted with each other to form the universe and life. These two principles were Prakriti and Purusha, the first representative of the world's underlying energy and the second its "ensouling" phenomenon, or spirit (in individuals and things). This led to a duality, as both Prakriti and Purusha were deemed eternal. In time, Purusha was beguiled by Prakriti's many potential material forms and ensouled itself in them. Individual souls became trapped in Prakriti. In other words, Purusha had *fallen* from its primordial capacity of soul. For "souls" to return to their former state of bliss, they were now enjoined to seek a path of renunciation of their embodied souls and fix their gaze on the purity of Purusha alone. In Ramacharaka's mind, these concepts preceded the period of the Greeks, their myths, and Plato, and lie behind all of Plato's separation between the physical realm and his realm of intellectual ascent.[6] Essentially, Plato adopted this Eastern idea that "evil" is the result of human ignorance and man's entrapment in the phenomenal world. Ramacharaka charges that Kapila was wrong to replace the pure realm of the ONE, ETERNAL THAT with a dualism that led to division and sorrow. To Ramacharaka's way of thinking, Plato and Western Christianity fell victim to this tragic line of reasoning.

It was only during the third period that the idea of unity resurfaced in the writings of the *Upanishads*, especially in their understanding of Brahman as the sole underlying reality of everything. In those commentaries, Vedanta "sprang into being," and India's philosophers began anew the task of codifying India's greatest truth: "that there is but One Reality, and that all the rest is illusory."[7] With the rise of the *Bhagavad Gita*, ways were finally offered for reunification with the ONE, or Brahman. In all of this, good and evil have to do with a *human fall*, as universal in Platonic thought as in the Bible and Sankhya lore. It is within this context that Ricoeur's interpretation of the Adamic and Orphic myths place God above good and evil.

Ricoeur's massive undertaking supersedes any full discussion here. What is significant for the present chapter is Ricoeur's interpretation of the Orphic myth vis-à-vis the Adamic myth. For Ricoeur, both accounts of the rise of evil and mankind's captivity in it were first expostulated in mythic form. Only later did the symbols yield to philosophical interpretation. The

---

5. Ibid., 53.
6. Ibid., 70.
7. Ibid., 85.

older Orphic myths were the first to separate man into "soul" and "body." Previous to that, Homer appears to have thought of mortals as having members, in contrast to a body, and whose soul was under the whimsical fate of gods. Orphism would alter this by placing 1) man's "soul" (*psyche*) into a "body" (*soma*), 2) whose soul had from eternity dwelt with God, and 3) for whom the "body" becomes a strange dwelling place, 4) leading to mankind's "forgetting of the difference" between soul and body.[8] With his soul divine and his body earthly, man's fate lies in struggling to regain his divine home. Aspects of this myth clearly echo Ramacharaka's description of the Sankhya system almost to a T. The body has become a prison house for a condemned "soul." Ecstatic rituals and mysteries reunite the "soul" with its "divine origin," much as Israel's "ecstatic prophets" experimented with a form of reunification with the divine (1 Sam 10:1–13). Ricoeur cites Plato's own comment on the Orphic "prison house" in Plato's dialogue *Cratylus*:

> It was the Orphics . . . who imposed that name [*soma*], in the belief that the soul atones for the faults for which it is punished and that, for its safekeeping, it has, round about it, the body in the likeness of a prison . . . the jail of the soul, until the soul has paid its debt . . .[9]

In Ricoeur's estimation, this Orphic myth combines the older tragic elements of Homeric myth, along with still older theogonic nuances of gods devouring each other, as in the case of the Titans who boiled and ate Dionysus. For that crime, Zeus struck them down and recreated mankind with a spark of Dionysus in him, as well as an element of Titanic evil.[10] Orphism, however, overcame this tragic condition by offering purifications as a reminder of man's true essence as divine. In doing so, Orphism revived the "old Indo-European theme of migration and reincarnation."[11] Plato would retain these elements as well, along with his critical view of the perishable physical world in contrast to the eternal orderly realm of Zeus.

Having traced the Orphic myth's evolution, Ricoeur turns to biblical Adam, in whose story he finds the more compelling explanation of good and evil. Keeping in mind that it too is an ancient myth, as well as a retroactively rewritten myth (dating from the time of the exile), Ricoeur praises the Adamic myth for clearly separating God from evil. God does not

8. Ricoeur, *Symbolism of Evil*, 280.
9. Ibid., 283.
10. Ibid., 285.
11. Ibid.

participate in Adam's "fall" at all. Nor is man part divine and partly human, but totally human. God breathes his breath (*ruah*) into the man (*adam*) made from the rich earth (*adama*), thus making him a living being. Adam is wholly mortal and possesses no divine status. It is only in the process of Adam's awakening to the powers within himself, that he elects to seize upon "the knowledge of good and evil" for himself, and, in so doing, unleashes a chain of consequences for which he alone is responsible.

By placing God beyond good and evil we spare ourselves a lifetime of self-victimization, in which we blame God, or some blind fate, for our human situation. By remembering that Genesis opens with a gracious Creator pronouncing creation "good," life is set before us as an exquisite wonder for self-fulfillment, actualization, and worthwhile goals. Thanks, also, to the New Testament's story of Christ's death and resurrection, or the Buddha's enlightened awakening to life as it is, religion provides an order of rebirth and deliverance, renewal and hope, with the power to lift human life forward, in spite of its own prison house of demeaning desires and culpable actions.

CHAPTER 9

The Ballast of Skepticism

Long before Socrates aroused from his slumbers to contest the rising skepticism of the Sophists of his time, the proclivity to question the existence of God was well established. The Greek playwrights had already drawn a dim view of the gods' capacity to bring justice out of chaos, or the power to reverse human tragedy. As Euripides' Hecuba is compelled to cry:

> Why call I on the Gods? They know, they know,
> My prayers, and would not hear them long ago.[1]

Skepticism was alive elsewhere too; and just as in Greece it was considered a crime against the state to denounce the gods, so also Israel's culture recoiled against YHWH's despisers. Its mockery of its own skeptics attests to the movement's presence and its demoralizing power. As the psalmist writes:

> The fool says in his heart: "There is no God."
> They are corrupt, they do abominable deeds,
> There is none that does good. (Ps 14:1–3)

For the most part, this "fool" (*nabal*) is called a "scoffer," or "sinner" in other places, because he refuses to conduct his life in accordance with YHWH's commandments (Ps 1). Therefore, his end will be marked by ruin and terror.

In spite of Israel's denouncement of his fate, however, that Israel mentions him speaks volumes. Deniers of God are found in all cultures. As in

---

1. Cited by Jones, *A History of Western Philosophy*, 21.

this "fool's" case, his own countrymen upbraid him. His skepticism and dismissive attitude of Israel's culture results in his being demonized by those who fear him. Because he has been demonized, we cannot know his true motives for rejecting God's existence or Israel's values. It is sufficient that the "fool" wants nothing to do with God or Israel. For whatever reasons, he is indifferent toward his nation's acquiescence in such a system; thus, he chooses to rebel against it. In Hebrew, his rejection originates "in his heart" (*belibbo*), in the very physiological and existential center of his being. The text wants us to believe that the "fool's" motives are anchored in his libertine, if not, blatant hedonism, but this may not be the case. As God looks down from heaven, he is forced to conclude "that there is none that does good, no, not one" (Ps 53:3). Indeed this "fool" has now become a prototype of "the sons of men," a representative of all. Even the Israelites' wisest men were forced now to acknowledge that belief in God and mankind's devotion to God meets with resistance. Far from faith being a natural, innate, and inner conviction, *faith has no ontological anchorage for many*. No Ground of Being speaks to them in their depths, or, if so, its voice carries no *hint of transcendence*. Nothing in their heart is motivated to seek that "Whom" they choose to deny. Perhaps this is its greatest threat to faith or belief in theism. Life is what it is, and we must each make the best of it however we can. No one can be forced to accept an Absolute. The "fool's" very existence forces Israel to reexamine its own normative principle: "Hear O Israel, the LORD our God, the LORD is one, and you shall love the LORD your God with all your heart . . . soul . . . and might" (Deut 6:4–5).

The "fool's" presence becomes a catalyst, jolting our understanding of reality. On the one hand, not everyone's experiences lead to faith. Why must religion degrade such persons? On the other hand, the "fool's" rebellion serves as an invitation for our own reevaluation of why we believe what we proclaim. It is a good lesson in epistemology. Even Anselm was forced to comment on the psalmist's "fool" in his *Proslogion*, as well as address the subject again in his *Reply to Gaunilo*. Gaunilo, a monk in a nearby monastery, had read Anselm's ontological argument with something of dismay. Thus, he responded that simply because a thing is in one's thought does not mean it exists in reality. Anslem's reply reechoed his conviction that as a thought, that which exists in the mind already enjoys an ontological existence; therefore to deny its existence would be "absurd." Writes Anselm:

> [So] let us suppose that it does not exist even though it can be thought. Now, whatever can be thought and does not

actually exist would not be, if it should exist, "that-than-which-a-greater-cannot-be-thought." If, therefore, it were "that-than-which-a-greater-cannot-be-thought" it would not be that-than-which-a-grater-cannot-be-thought, which is completely absurd.[2]

It is only when we turn to Paul Tillich's *A Complete History of Christian Thought* that Anselm's reply is elucidated more clearly. In his typical philosophical manner, Tillich comments:

> God is identical . . . with the experience of the unconditional as true . . . and good. What the ontological argument really does is to analyze in human thought something unconditional, which transcends subjectivity and objectivity. The . . . argument is a phenomenological description of the human mind, insofar as the human mind by necessity points to something beyond [itself] and points to the experience of truth.[3]

In the final analysis, the psalmist's "fool" may represent nothing more than a thoughtless victim of his own karma, a soul enmeshed in the chains of samsara that he has created for himself. Even so, as a skeptic, he is entitled to reject a theistic view of the universe if it fails to engender existential import for his life. That may gall some, but the *nabal* in all of us is capable of learning something about ourselves from faith's skeptics, resulting in a reexamination of whatever truths we hold most dear.

Gaunilo's uneasiness with Anselm's dismissal of the psalmist's "fool" may have enjoyed a quaint and marginal, if not brief, tenure throughout the remaining years of the medieval period, but with the dawn of the modern era, Hume would reopen all the wounds of the skeptics' misgivings.

In his *Dialogue Concerning Natural Religion*, Hume's primary objection rests on his oft-repeated conviction that "similar causes prove similar effects, and similar effects similar causes."[4] Or again, "cause ought only be proportioned to the effect."[5] Or "like effects arise from like causes," or, expressed in still another way: "where several known circumstances are observed to be similar, the unknown will also be found similar."[6] The *Dialogue* pits three interlocutors against each other, though in a genteel and pleasant

---

2. Anselm, *Major Works, Reply to Gaunilo*, 112.
3. See Tillich, *Complete History of Christian Thought*, 164.
4. See Hick's *Classical and Contemporary Readings*, 72–73.
5. Ibid., 82.
6. Ibid., 85.

fashion. Hume's own position is championed by a certain Philo, while adherents to the design argument and to natural theology (that God's perfection and being are visible and deducible from the observation of nature) are represented by Cleanthes and Demea. Hume's Philo proves relentless in picking holes in his comrades' positions.

Echoing Gaunilo's objection to Anselm's ontological argument, Philo insists that: "our ideas reach no farther than our experience. We have no experience of divine attributes and operations," thus whatever the mind conceives as an attribute of God's may not be the case at all. "[Let] us beware lest we think that our ideas anywise correspond to His perfections, or that His attributes have any resemblance to these qualities among men."[7] This second principle is as important for Hume as his first: "that like effects require only like causes." On this basis, Hume's Philo goes on to eviscerate the so-called design argument, for from the effects of creation and the behavior of mankind, it is impossible to prove that an infinite, powerful, intelligent, and all-loving Being created the universe. If anything, the contrary appears to be true. When both Cleanthes and Demas contend that: "religion, however corrupted, is still better than no religion at all," Philo recoils at the suggestion and reminds both of the "pernicious consequences . . . factions, civil wars, persecutions, subversions of government, oppression, and slavery" that religion has caused across the years. No, he will not cede a single thread of credibility in his rebuttal to their views. If anything, "the terrors of religion commonly prevail above its comforts."[8] What is so remarkable about Hume's critique is that it foreshadows and contains all the major equivocations that his successors have argued since him, including Bertrand Russell and Richard Dawkins. Then in something of a paradoxical twist, Hume's Philo concludes that a "person, seasoned with a just sense of the imperfections of natural reason, will fly to revealed truth with the greatest avidity."[9] In this unexpected conclusion, Hume appears to be taunting his own agnosticism, which Kant picked up on, and pursued with his own critique of philosophy and religion.

We have already reviewed Kant's important distinction between analytic and synthetic propositions, or judgments of necessity versus judgments of experience. On that basis, there exists no empirical evidence for the existence of God; only a transcendental one, as discussed in chapter 4.

7. Ibid., 69.
8. Ibid., 104.
9. Ibid., 106.

In part, Kant reached this conclusion based on his so-called Copernican Revolution, which he mentions in the preface to his second edition of his *Critique of Pure Reason*. Rather than assuming, as Hume had, that "our knowledge must conform to objects," he wondered whether metaphysics would not enjoy more success if it argued that "objects must conform to our knowledge."[10] By this he meant that the mind imposes certain a priori categories on the phenomena it processes. Example, the mind invariably judges things to be categorical, hypothetical, or disjunctive. It does this with all judgments it makes. It also judges modes of quality as real, non-real, or limited. Observed objects must pass through this sieve of *Vernunft* (i.e., the way the mind reasons) for *Sinnlichkeit,* (or sensations) to be perceived.[11] Since God is not an observable phenomenon, nor is the soul, neither can be processed as a phenomenon of the world. They can only be posited as transcendental ideas. They cannot be proven as things-in-themselves.

Kant would apply his method of *Vernunft* to the so-called arguments for the existence of God (the ontological, cosmological, and argument from design), contending that none was anything more than an analytical judgment and therefore a non-empirical proposition without existential value. In doing so he paved the way for philosophers such as Karl Marx and Ludwig Feuerbach to conceive of religion as an opiate of the masses or as a projection of our finite individuality purified and objectified as the infinite, almighty, loving God. Following on their heels was the soon-to-become most acerbic voice of their time: Friedrich Nietzsche.

Until Nietzsche, and possibly Schopenhauer, Europe's commanding figures of philosophy had based their central metaphysical concepts and ethics on elements of Western Christianity and its Neoplatonic roots. Not so with Nietzsche. He drew his inspiration from the Greek classics. More so than most, Nietzsche's philosophy takes on the role of oracular discontent with both philosophical investigation and Western Christianity. Passion replaces reason in the form of Dionysus and aesthetic restraint in the form of Apollo. The cold ascent of deductive logic, guided by the past, has brought metaphysics to an end with its sterile themes of subjectivism and objectivism. In Nietzsche's mind, the West needed a new myth by which to live and reason. He established such in *The Birth of Tragedy*, in which the vitalistic and darker passions of the god Dionysus reawakened his followers' lives, while the god Apollo appealed for restraint, lest their ecstatic

---

10. See Kant, *Critique of Pure Reason*, 375.
11. Ibid., 396.

natures destroy their promise of a meaningful existence. Nietzsche's is a poetic approach, a metaphorical commentary on existence, as much as it is a reasoned critique of philosophy's purpose. It is under this guise as a poet of existence that Nietzsche proclaims his criticism of religion. Moreover, it is from this perspective that he unites his theme of the *will to power*, on the one hand, with the coming of the *Overman* or *Superman* (*der Übermensch*), on the other, or his theme of nihilism with his call for courage. His is a philosophy of exuberance tempered by the "know thyself" of Apollo.

For Nietzsche, classical man could not have survived without recognizing elements of Dionysus and Apollo in himself; nor are we any different.

> Whoever approaches these Olympians with another religion in his heart, searching among them for moral elevation, even for sanctity, for disincarnate spirituality, for charity and benevolence, will soon be forced to turn his back on them, discouraged and disappointed. For there is nothing here that suggests asceticism, spirituality, or duty. We hear nothing but the accents of an exuberant, triumphant life in which all things, . . . are deified . . . .[12]

> Apollo, as ethical deity, exacts measure of his disciples, and, to be able to maintain it, he requires self-knowledge. And so, side by side with the aesthetic necessity for beauty, there occur the demands "know thyself" and "nothing in excess." . . . The effects wrought by the Dionysian also seemed "titanic" and "barbaric" to the Apollinian Greek; while at the same time he could not conceal from himself that he, too, was inwardly related to these overthrown Titans and heroes. Indeed, he had to recognize even more that this: despite all its beauty and moderation, his entire existence rested on a hidden substratum of suffering and of knowledge revealed to him by the Dionysian. . . . Apollo could not live without Dionysus! The "titanic" and "barbaric" were . . . as necessary as the Apollinian.[13]

These critical quotes enable us to understand why Nietzsche propounded the idea of the death of God. In addition, since he considered Western metaphysics and its Kantian transcendentalism equally dead, Nietzsche turned to the "will to power," or life's underlying Dionysian exuberance, to found a new metaphysics. In his *On the Genealogy of Morals*, he denounces Christianity's "doctrine of resentment" for weakening mankind's resolve to address real issues. Such a morality has only made man "weaker,"

---

12. Nietzsche, *Birth of Tragedy*, 41.
13. Ibid., 46.

"contemptuous," filling him with a "vengeful cunning of impotence."[14] Only someone of an "ascetic ideal," who dares to think and act for himself can lead the way toward a new future. That "ideal" is the *Übermensch*, whom Zarathustra extols, and whom Nietzsche holds up as mankind's prototype of redemption.[15]

> *I teach you the Superman.* Man is something that should be overcome. What have you done to overcome him? . . . What is the ape to men? A laughing-stock or a painful embarrassment. And just so shall man be to the Superman. . . . Behold, I teach you the Superman. [He] is the meaning of the earth. Let your will say: The Superman shall be the meaning of the earth! . . .[16]
>
> I welcome all signs that a more virile, warlike age is about to begin, which will restore honor to courage above all. For this age shall prepare the way for one yet higher . . . that will carry heroism into the search for knowledge and that will *wage wars* for the sake of ideas and their consequences. To this end we need many preparatory courageous human beings . . . who are bent on seeking in all things for what in them must be *overcome* . . . .[17]

In conjunction with the will to power and the necessity of the Overman, Nietzsche revitalized the myth of the eternal return. No heaven or hell awaits anyone, only a loneliest loneliness that one must face everyday, doing so in the knowledge that each day requires one to affirm life anew, making the most of it as best one can. No one else can do that for you. It is such a striking metaphor out of the depths that it deserves viewing.

> What, if some day or night a demon were to steal after you into your loneliest loneliness and say to you: "This life as you now live it and have lived it, you will have to live once more and innumerable times more; and there will be nothing new in it, but every pain and every joy and every thought and sigh and everything unutterably small or great in your life will have to return to you . . . ?"[18]

Something of Hinduism and Buddhism's cycles of samsara haunts this passage, but Nietzsche's reference to its "sighs" and "pains" drops us instantly into the psalmist's abyss again. For all Nietzsche's vision, mankind

---

14. Nietzsche, *On the Genealogy of Morals*, 46.
15. Ibid., 41–43.
16. Ibid., 42.
17. See Nietzsche, *Gay Science*, 228.
18. Ibid., 273.

is still faced with its own "depths," which heretofore only God could fill. The "depths" remain. The lonely, empty gap is still present, just as it is in all systems that seek to elude or deny the mystery of God. How to fill it still remains a challenge, whether the solution is interpreted as the Tao, the Übermensch, Brahman, or the Buddha-essence.

In more recent years, the late Bertrand Russell continued to champion modern philosophy's discontent with religious solutions. In his iconoclastic *Why I Am Not a Christian*, he joined Hume in asking why human beings can't stop their enquiries with nature itself, rather than having to posit an Uncaused Causer, an Unmoved Mover, and Necessary Being. As early as his youth, he tells us that he came to the conclusion that appealing to God in order to explain the universe gets us nowhere, for if everything has to have a cause, then why not God himself? Moreover, he questioned the New Testament's portrait of Jesus, suggesting that the Jesus it preserves hardly comes across as the wisest or best of all human beings. Many of his dismissals have the air of a bright, English schoolboy enjoying his deflation of a literalist's naïve faith. In doing so, he is most effective. Nevertheless, the issues he raises remain problematic to this day. Like Hume, he finds parts of the church still prejudiced, blind to reason, hostile to science, intolerant of open-minded reasonableness, indifferent to suffering, and content to emphasize the "soul" and "immortality" over the social ills of the world. By "emphasizing the soul, Christian ethics has made itself completely individualistic." So too its doctrine of immortality has turned its focus away from the evils and cruelties of time with "disastrous effects upon morals" and in metaphysics an equally disastrous effect on philosophy.[19]

Russell's more philosophical objections, however, are reserved for his *Principia Mathematica*. Russell labeled his position "Logical Atomism." He wanted to create a system of analyzing language on the basis of its relationship to "facts." Statements should represent "facts" as accurately as possible. Moreover, the truth or falsehood of a statement is a function of the truth or falsehood of its component words or simplest "atomic" parts. Since God is not a "fact" in any empirical sense, propositions about God possess a very low level of "veracity," if any at all.[20] A history of the movement Russell's atomism inspired can be traced through the schools of Logical Positivism, Analytic Philosophy, and the works of Wittgenstein.[21] The movement's

---

19. Russell, *Why I Am Not a Christian*, 35.
20. See Stumpf, *Philosophy*, 449–51.
21. Ibid., 446–80.

impact on theology has taken its toll. The study of systematic theology has often had to yield to histories of theology, and even superseding these have been the continual quests of the historical Jesus, such as the Catholic scholar John Dominic Crossan represents. Far from viewing Jesus as the second person of the Trinity, in many instances today's New Testament scholars portray Jesus as a peasant sage in the tradition of a Greek Cynic. The Gospels do not so much provide us with a biography of the Jesus of history but represent retroactive revisions iterated into his elusive life. In the same way that the Jewish community of the exile read its own history back into the Adamic myth, so the early church read its interpretations of Jesus' life into its Gospels. Even the Buddhist scholar, Sangharakshita, in his *The Three Jewels: An Introduction to Modern Buddhism*, acknowledges that similar developments have resulted in quests of the historical Buddha among Buddhists themselves.[22] But Russell did not mince any words concerning Buddhists priests either: "The Buddha was amiable and enlightened. . . . But the Buddhist priesthood . . . has been obscurantist, tyrannous, and cruel in the highest degree."[23] In the final analysis, Russell concludes: "I regard [religion] as a disease born of fear and as a source of untold misery to the human race."[24] Russell is dead, but many of the doctrines and conditions he strove to correct are, unfortunately, still alive.

In more recent years, Richard Dawkins of Oxford University has taken up the mantle as the latest chief skeptic of religion. He is especially opposed to any form of "supernaturalism," or belief in the monotheistic God of Christianity, Judaism, and Islam. He describes himself as a genuine atheist who is opposed to the propagation of God in any form. With Wilson of Harvard, he considers science to be at war with religion as the most "common form of superstition."[25] He makes it clear: "I decry supernaturalism in all its forms. . . . I am not attacking any particular version of God or gods. I am attacking God, all gods, anything and everything supernatural, wherever and whenever they have been or will be invented."[26] Unfortunately, this passionate, evangelical mission—which he assumes in the name of science—detracts from many of his arguments, as it interjects an emotional and combative attitude that belies the "truths of objectivity"

22. Sangharakshita, *Three Jewels*, 44f.
23. Russell, *Why I Am Not a Christian*, 25.
24. Ibid., 24.
25. Dawkins, *God Delusion*, 92.
26. Ibid., 57.

he seeks to establish. He is especially committed to a number of principles that underlie his position. Although he doesn't list them in any particular order, they appear and reappear throughout his book, *The God Delusion*:

1) That only scientific propositions are capable of verification. 2) That the propositions of theologians, therefore, are without truth-value, inasmuch as they cannot be verified. 3) The same may be said about the so-called NOMA theory, i.e., the *non-overlapping magisterial* hypothesis which affirms that the "*magisterium* of science covers the empirical realm," while that of religion "extends over questions of ultimate meaning and moral value."[27] That 4) Darwin's theory of natural selection and evolution, along with modern astronomy's grasp of the universe's origin, provides the only required ingredients we need for understanding ourselves and our universe; 5) that although science can never totally disprove the existence of God, given what we know above, it is highly *improbable* that God exists; therefore, 6) the continued belief in a supernatural God who sustains and guides the universe is totally at variance with the truth as we know it.

Dawkins devotes a central portion of his thought to criticizing Intelligence Design and its "creationist" supporters. Evolution and natural selection, over billions of years of time, are sufficient to account for the incremental and "improbable" changes that led to life as we know it on Earth. Thus, the creationists' appeal to any God-of-the-gaps or the necessity of an intelligent Designer to account for the Earth's complex fauna and flora fails to solve the problem of spontaneous creation. States Dawkins:

> Creationist "logic" is always the same. Some natural phenomenon is too statistically improbable, too complex, too beautiful, too awe-inspiring to have come into existence by chance.... Therefore a designer must have done it. And science's answer to this faulty logic is also always the same. Design is not the only alternative to chance. Natural selection is a better alternative. Indeed, design is not a real alternative at all because it raises an even bigger problem than it solves: who designed the designer? ... Natural selection is a real solution. It is the only workable solution that has ever been suggested. And it is not only a workable solution, it is a solution of stunning elegance and power.[28]

Along the way, Dawkins resuscitates the foreboding charges that Hume and Russell leveled at Western Christianity. God, as that "interventionist,

---

27. Ibid., 78f.
28. Ibid., 146–47.

THE BALLAST OF SKEPTICISM

miracle-wreaking, thought-reading, sin-punishing, prayer-answering God of the Bible, of priests, mullahs, and rabbis" is simply a "pernicious delusion."[29] As for the capacity of theologians to critique, add to, or elucidate the God Hypothesis, one should scorn the thought: "I don't think we should throw them . . . a sop. I have yet to see any good reason to suppose that theology . . . is a subject at all."[30] As Dawkins enjoys reminding his readers: "An atheist in [the] sense of [being a] philosophical naturalist is somebody who believes there is nothing beyond the natural, physical world, no *super*natural creative intelligence lurking behind the observable universe, no soul that outlasts the body and no miracles."[31] He also insists that, far from debunking the arts and beauty, an atheist, as a "naturalist" holds each in high regard. Quoting a fellow atheist, he writes:

> What most atheists do believe is that although there is only one kind of stuff in the universe and it is physical, out of this stuff come minds, beauty, emotions, moral values, in short the full gamut of phenomena that gives richness to human life.[32]

Of course, at this point, Dawkins has ceased to be a scientist and has become a metaphysician without realizing it. His statement about "beauty, emotions, moral value . . . that give[s] richness to human life" is a *judgment*, not just an *observation*, and, as such, begs for a criterion, which his empiricism cannot justify.

Nonetheless, Dawkins' critique offers many convincing points, but his crusade to stamp out as much belief in God as possible entraps him in the very web of intolerance he accuses of others. This extends both to his definition of God as well as his usage of ad hominem, ad populum, and other fallacies that abound in his book. To use Thomas Jefferson, whose Deist views he rejects, as an authority against religion is hardly justifiable, let alone objective. So also his one-sided definition of God strains credulity. Granted, as a biologist, his primary focus is concentrated on disproving the fundamentalist views of creationists; nevertheless, for enlightened Christians—if we may call them so—his failure to address the question of mankind's experience of the depths, or counter Paul Tillich's theory of the Ground of Being, or mention Schleiermacher's sense of absolute

---

29. Ibid., 41, 52.
30. Ibid., 80.
31. Ibid., 35.
32. Ibid., 34.

dependence of the finite upon the Infinite minimizes his refutation's impact. There are far more profound issues at stake than creating a straw man, or straw God, who nobody in their right mind would ever worship. But then his view of theology excuses him from having to address the questions of transcendence and self-awareness. Even more telling is the absence of any references to the keenest philosophical minds of our age: Whitehead, Marcel, Heidegger, and Hartshorne, all of whom wrestled with degrees of transcendence. Indeed, in Whitehead's terms, Dawkins is arrested at the level of "God the enemy." That is a horrible thing to charge, but Dawkins' approach places him at that level.

Nonetheless, having said this, Dawkins' salient points constitute a viable critique of religion. He compels us to ask what purpose an *improbably existing God* plays in the formation of our universe and our own lives. If a non-caused, spontaneous Big Bang did fling out all the ingredients necessary to our universe, including our own creation over time, what possible essential role would remain for a God like YHWH or Allah to play? In Dawkins' view, none! But what if God isn't that process-abandoning, hands-off deity, or absentee-creation lord Dawkins imagines him to be? What if God is more like Hartshorne's "dual transcendent" deity that innerves the universe, comes to consciousness in our own cellular stuff (as an inescapable other), and elicits our response in terms of wonder, love, and gratitude? The naturalist in Dawkins is much closer to that "God" than he is to the intelligent Designer that, in his view, the universe cannot support. As David Hume bemoaned: O how even the most hardened naturalist would flee with avidity toward the revelation of such a Source!

CHAPTER 10

The Dynamics of Doubt and Its Anodyne Faith

SCIENTIFIC AS WELL AS philosophical objections to the existence of God are nothing new. It is the doubt they generate that requires attention. Biblical Adam is but one example of doubt's innervating power as his heart sank into the mire of existential default. The more Adam pondered the extent to which he ought exercise his personal freedom, the further he removed himself from God's influence. We shall come back to him, but a number of universal characteristics deserve mention first.

Paul Tillich, in his *Dynamics of Faith*, began his probe with an analysis of doubt. He referred to it as "existential doubt," or that doubt that underlies our entire relationship with the self and the world. It is an inescapable facet of human existence, in so far as it witnesses to an uneasy ontological precondition that accompanies all thought and action. Unlike scientific doubt—such as Hume, Russell, and Dawkins embrace—existential doubt already lies behind the scientist's concern for verification, for which even verification can never satisfy. Tillich refers to scientific doubt as "methodological doubt," a necessary aspect of "empirical inquiry or logical deduction." However, Tillich warns that a "scientist who would say that a scientific theory is beyond doubt would at that moment cease to be scientific."[1] Little wonder that Hume longed to fly with avidity toward a Source that would cure his existential doubt, or that Dawkins at least expresses a willingness to mention the *probability* of the existence of God. Being wed, however, to his

1. Tillich, *Dynamics of Faith*, 19.

scientific convictions and their materialistic basis, the improbability of God strikes him as more feasible than God's existence. Nonetheless, Dawkins' existential doubt ripples as a strong undercurrent throughout his refutation of Intelligent Design.

Tillich acknowledges a second form of existential doubt, which he labels: "skeptical doubt." It is an "attitude toward all the beliefs of man, from sense experiences to religious creeds." It results in "actually rejecting any certainty," thus it leads to despair, cynicism, intolerance, and, finally, indifference.[2]

Religious doubt leads to a host of other, concomitant conditions. Once God is edged out of the space that only God can fill, new marks of the human condition hold sway: guilt, abandonment, and estrangement to name but a few. All these conditions appear as universal consequences of doubt in the old Adamic myth (Gen 2–3), which preceded the Priestly writers' post-exilic reinterpretation (Gen 1). In that older myth, stages of the couple's doubt emerge, first as guilt and then as abandonment, and, finally, as estrangement. All this is symbolized in the story of their "nakedness," or vulnerability and flight from YHWH's presence. The writer clearly understood the reality of mankind's "existential doubt," though the term would have mystified him. Nonetheless, he understood its nuance quite well, as he depicts God walking through the Garden in the quiet of the evening, demanding: "Where are you?" (Gen 3:9). Quickly, the couple sought to cover up their nakedness, to disguise it, but their consciences balked. Consequently it led to profound *remorse*, for they could never be innocent again; then to *recrimination*, as they fell into faulting one another; and finally *estrangement*, as they were hastily conducted from the idyllic paradise of Eden.

To his credit, the Yahwist crafted the drama with deft precision, as he envisioned God ordering the *Angel of the Lord* to drive them out, and to do so with a *sword*, lest they eat of the Tree of Life and *live forever*. Eternity belongs only to God and secondarily to his host of shimmering beings. Mankind's rebellious nature must now endure the limits of his finitude, with all the vicissitudes of existence. Wherever he goes, whatever he adventures, will be marked by uncertainty. His access to the "garden of potentiality" comes only at great price. His existentiality invades his deepest sense of self, preceding all he ponders or might achieve. It will temper everything he attempts to actualize or dream.

2. Ibid.

In a less philosophical vein, other conditions surface as well. Certainly, the loss of naïveté plays a factor. As one matures and reflects on cherished convictions, one's "first naïveté" undergoes assault. Any student of today's study of religion can identify with the sinking feeling that seizes one upon realizing that the Jesus of the Gospels represents at best only a construct of the Evangelists, whose views in turn were based on inadequate historical verification. Indeed, as New Testament scholarship peels back the layers of Jesus' time and place, along with its political and religious underpinnings, one's naïve belief in Jesus as the Son of God, descended from heaven to die for human sin, begins to waver. Marcus Borg, a prominent New Testament scholar, explains how his own naïveté was shaken upon experiencing the same. In his case, however, the loss of "first naïveté" led to a deeper, more profound, and constructive appreciation of Christ's meaning. His *Meeting Jesus Again for the First Time* traces his story for like-minded believers to read.[3]

The loss of naïveté, however, does not always result in a more profound grasp of God. It can lead to "anguish, despair, and forlornness," such as Camus and Sartre chose to address. In their daring leap to embrace the absurd, they challenged compatriots to *shape* their own futures, free of the past and its metaphysical baggage. In their view, there is no absolute nature to which we must conform but only a history that we are entitled to write for ourselves. To fail to do so is to lapse into bad faith—*mauvaise foi*. Anguish will always be part of an existential life, with its necessity to choose for oneself. To fail to make your own choices is to lapse into a life defined by others. In his *Being and Nothingness*, Sartre addressed two forms of being: being-in-itself (*être-en-soi*) and being-for-itself (*être-pour-soi*). A rock can never be more than a rock, but a human being can define or shape his or her own destiny. This is true even when under duress, for one can at least choose to say, "*Non!*"

Nowhere does Sartre popularize his existentialism with greater clarity than in his work *Existentialism*. Willing to reject "the Christian standpoint" and "God's commandments and . . . eternal verities," Sartre maps out his own position with unflinching remorselessness:

> Atheistic existentialism, which I represent, . . . states that if God does not exist, there is at least one being in whom existence precedes essence, a being who exists before he can be defined by any concept, and that this being is man. . . . It means, first of all, that

---

3. See Borg, *Meeting Jesus Again*, 3ff.

man exists, turns up, appears on the scene, and only afterwards, defines himself. . . . Thus there is no human nature, since there is no God to conceive it. Not only is man what he conceives himself to be, but he is also only what he wills himself to be after this thrust towards existence. . . . [He] is nothing else but what he makes of himself.[4]

Sartre goes on to explain why such an existence must assert the courage to accept "anguish, forlornness, and despair." 1) *Anguish*, because one's choices require a responsibility that one can no longer lay to anyone else. 2) *Forlornness*, because if "God does not exist . . . we have to face all the consequences of this" by ourselves. It further means that there can "no longer be an *a priori* Good."[5] For "we are alone with no excuses . . . condemned to be free."[6] And 3) *despair*, because everything falls on man. There exists no outside world to which to appeal. "[Man] is nothing else than a series of undertakings, that he is the sum, the organization, the ensemble of the relationships which make up [his] undertakings." There is no alternative that is going to rescue him. It means, "that I shall have no illusions and shall do what I can."[7]

In his short story entitled "The Wall," he depicts a group of imprisoned freedom fighters opposed to Franco during the Spanish Civil War. They are held in a dank room, awaiting their execution. Each man squirms at the thought of being the next prisoner called. Only one prisoner, who acknowledges that there are no values that govern life, is prepared to "die clean."

> Time was running out. . . . Little Juan was beginning to cry . . . "I don't want to die. I don't' want to die. I don't want to die." . . . I could clearly see he was pitying himself. . . . I said to myself, "I want to die cleanly." . . . I heard shots at almost regular intervals; I shook with each one of them. I wanted to scream and tear out my hair. But I gritted my teeth . . . because I wanted to stay clean.[8]

Later the hero is asked if he wouldn't like to reveal the whereabouts of their leader's hiding place. They will set him free if he will only betray his friend. But he refuses and reflects to himself: "It was not for this reason that

---

4. See Sartre's "Existentialism is a Humanism," 521.
5. Ibid., 522–23.
6. Ibid., 524.
7. Ibid., 526.
8. Ibid., 516–17.

I consented to die in his place; his life had no more value than mine; no life had value." After further reflection, he tells himself "I must be stubborn."[9]

Sartre's story requires mentioning if for no other reason than its contrast with Plato's prisoners, chained to their "wall" of deception and darkness. Plato chooses to rescue his prisoners, to deliver them from darkness into light, while Sartre (at least in a literary sense) mocks the *mauvaise foi* of "Little Juan," who begs not to die. Existential doubt brings every man or woman to his/her moment of truth. For Sartre, to "die clean" is preferable to believing in something you cannot accept. Religion needs his voice when it betrays the Ultimate for anything less.

Philosophers and scientists are not the only ones to prefer the Void over faith. Who cannot help but identify with Thomas Hardy or Matthew Arnold when faced with their moment of truth?

The Oxen

Christmas Eve, and twelve of the clock.
    "Now they are all on their knees,"
An elder said as we sat in a flock
    By the embers in hearthside ease.

We pictured the meek mild creatures where
    They dwelt in their strawy pen,
Nor did it occur to one of us there
    To doubt they were kneeling then.

So fair a fancy few would weave
    In these years! Yet, I feel,
If someone said on Christmas Eve,
    "Come, see the oxen kneel

"In the lonely barton by yonder coomb
    Our childhood used to know,"
I should go with him in the gloom,
    Hoping it might be so.[10]

---

9. Ibid., 518.
10. Thomas Hardy, "The Oxen."

In the final analysis, Tillich argues that doubt can only be overcome by faith, which in turn requires risk and courage. Sartre's desire to "die clean" represents his commensurate risk and act of courage to accept existence, as he understood it. So also Camus' decision to embrace the Absurd. For Tillich, "faith is the state of being ultimately concerned." Most of us are caught up in "urgent concerns," but these can never replace the "ultimate." And only that can be "ultimate" that demands our total surrender while promising our total fulfillment.[11] That alone is God, the Ground of Being, in Tillich's mind, who alone can demand the loyalty of one's whole existence and alone fulfill the longings of humankind's existentiality. In that respect, God represents both the void and the dread that accompany mankind's quest of wholeness, until man rests his case in Whitehead's supreme Companion.

Such cannot happen without its moments of uncertainty, anguish, and misgivings. It is why Søren Kierkegaard's *Fear and Trembling* still resonates with many readers. In the Dane's thrice-told story of Abraham's journey to Mt. Moriah, where the patriarch has been summoned to offer Isaac as a sacrifice, Kierkegaard confronts believers with the realization of how incommunicable and anxiety filled a life of faith truly is. For Kierkegaard, there can be no substitute for it, if one's faith is to be genuine and one's surrender to the Absolute an absolute surrender. A relative relationship with the Eternal will never do; only an absolute relationship with the Absolute conquers doubt. In his *Philosophical Fragments*, he goes even further. Of what advantage, if any, did Jesus' first disciples enjoy over others? he asks. Did they too not have to make their own leaps of faith with fear and trembling just as the contemporary disciple must do? Faith is not without its anxiety, its moments of silence and anguish. Yet faith in God alone is the final and only answer to mankind's destitution, or "error," as Kierkegaard labels it.[12]

Hinduism cherishes the same. It does not matter which of the four paths, or yogas, a devotee follows, whether the path of knowledge, duty, devotion, or mysticism, as long as one does so with "single-minded devotion." Zen requires the same. For only those haunted by the "ultimate" truly pass through the "Gateless Gate," whereupon afterwards they may walk freely in the universe. Nor is the way of Buddhism strikingly different. It is only when one wakes up, and sets aside one's inordinate self-consciousness and embraces life's impermanence, that one can address world suffering.

---

11. Tillich, *Dynamics*, 1.
12. Kierkegaard, *Philosophical Fragments*, 81.

Kierkegaard adds an interesting wrinkle, however, to his analysis of faith. In the *Philosophical Fragments* he raises the question of how one comes to faith. Even the disciple at first hand had to experience something to arouse his faith. Kierkegaard refers to this as the "Moment," or the "occasion," which awakens the disciple to the reality of the Absolute. Since man is incapable of providing this "Moment" for himself, whence its source? For the disciples, the "Moment" was occasioned by the presence of Christ, a gift of grace that they could never have invented or willed on their own. So, too, the contemporary disciple stands in equal need of that "Moment," which only God can provide. That engagement or moment can come at any time whenever the "eternal condition is given in time."[13] It may come in Scripture, or in a believer's coming face-to-face with the truth about himself as he stands before the miracle of Christ; however, there is no such thing as faith at "second hand." All coming to faith requires the "Moment" before God, in which one either falls dizzily backwards into his or her existential despair or makes his leap of faith in the Absolute. Abraham chose the latter as did Jesus' disciples.

It is not the place of religion, or Christianity in particular, to fault Hawking, Wilson, or Dawkins' choice. Each has done so in an effort to resolve his existential doubt as Truth's "Moment" has come to him. For that, each is to be admired, but their presuppositions and data, along with their empirical method, are not beyond philosophical criticism. That is why faith in God remains a compelling option for believers whose presuppositions include the possibility of God's existence. It is not for science to mock or devalue this human right, cherished as a "right" by most nations around the world, anymore than it is for religion to dismiss the hard-sought revelations of science as if the latter were falsely acquired.

13. Ibid.

CHAPTER 11

Redemption and Redeemers

IN THE LIGHT OF what we know about contemporary mankind (its behavior and inherited biological code, cultural grounding, and susceptibility to modern disorders), doctrines of sacrifice and expiation seem woefully out of order as pathways of "redemption" for our time. Such doctrines appear more anchored in the ancient world and its sense of helplessness before the machinations of nature than appropriate for human salvation today. However elaborate and rich the ritual employed to persuade and appease the unknown powers to guarantee safety and fertility, earlier mankind's lives still fell victim to the demoralizing perplexities that lay before them. In addition to the numerous uncertainties of the cyclical vagaries of the seasons that humans from the Stone Age to ancient Greece faced, they were equally haunted by their personal misgivings and failure to cope with life's enigmas and sorrows, including their own culpable activities. Salvation cults emerged across the ancient Near East even late into the time of the Roman Empire. Because of the terror and severity of life's vagaries, priests were prone to answer with the harshest of remedies, often in the form of self-abasement just shy of human sacrifice. We know that as late as the time of the Roman Republic, Carthaginians were still practicing child sacrifice. The Mystery Religions of the Empire itself witnessed to the rise of many salvation cults, in which the dying and rising of a savior god was central. This puts redeemer and redemption religions of the juristic type at a definite crossroads in our time. Contemporary humanity's concern for wholeness and freedom from disillusionment, self-indulgent emptiness, and a general sense of meaninglessness requires a far more holistic approach than ancient expiation.

One might argue that, from a philosophical perspective, redemption religions face both a formative and material barrier that requires investigation. From a *formative* viewpoint, the idea of God as an avenger, who demands a sacrifice greater than which man can provide, or which threatens his very life, or that of his sons or daughters, introduces a bifurcation in God in favor of God's darker side. This constitutes a formative error, inasmuch as it depicts the Ground of Being as man's enemy rather than man's source of vitality, fortitude, reclamation, and hope. It has nothing to do with God. Its emergence lies in mankind's thwarted attempt to appease the harsher realities of his own existence, his fear and guilt, as well as his failure to manipulate his weaker fellowman, or avoid being harassed by them. The religions of taboo and human sacrifice across the ages reflect this error. As one beyond good and evil, to conceive of God as a jealous, punitive, or bloodthirsty deity, whose ego must be forever pacified and whose existence and values demand total capitulation is unworthy of any concept of God. Such forensic or punishment-based redemptions scarcely witness to divine love, transcendence, or the possibility of transformation.

From a *material* perspective, equally daunting objections arise. Regardless of their content, such religions appeal more to mankind's fear and/or self-righteousness than to uplifting principles that might assist one to overcome *remorse* and *alienation*, the latter two being essential in any concept of redemption. Consequently, such appeals cast aspersions on God's Being, whether such religions portray God as Brahman, the Holy Trinity, Allah, or the Buddha Essence. If the Gospels' depictions of Jesus are in anyway accurate, he rejected appeals to self-righteousness or vengeance. His own injunctions and references to God are guided by principles more in common with Whitehead "God as Companion" and Hartshorne's "Dual Transcendence" than Evangelical views of guilt and damnation, requiring repentance and faith in order to gain Eternity. That Jesus was willing to forgive "sin" was the central point. We are already embedded in the Eternal Now, conscious of the Divine Ground of Being from which we cannot flee (Ps 139).

If this critique is correct, or warrants any level of feasibility, what corrective measures might be offered vis-à-vis redemption religions and/or their respective redeemers? Let us begin with a definition of redemption more attune to contemporary human needs. As such, one might define redemption as *the cost of recovering one's freedom from one's failure to address life's existential bondage (of finitude, doubt, and meaninglessness) and one's proclivity to act against one's highest sense of will, traditionally regarded as "rebellion" against God in the Judeo-Christian religions*. This more than anything else explains mankind's sense of *alienation*, from himself and his neighbor, and, above all, from God. The history of religion is replete with redeemers who have led the way to such deliverance. Among them is Israel's Suffering Servant, the dying and rising Christ of the Gospels, the descending avatars of Vishnu, the Bodhisattvas of Buddhism, and the saintly sadhus of India. Even Islam's Mohammed qualifies as a gateway of redemption insofar as his life and prophetic recitations claim the Muslim's allegiance to the One alone who bestows *salam* or peace.

From a modern perspective, mankind's redeemers can be viewed as avenues of awareness of man's existential forfeiture that must be acknowledged and addressed. As such, redemption incorporates a number of legitimate factors: 1) ownership of one's fragmented condition, whether due to existential doubt, the fear of nonbeing, or the specter of meaninglessness, 2) recognition of a need for reclamation from one's own harmful and debilitating behavior, 3) the identification of one's condition with select historical figures as providers and exemplars of enlightenment and transcendence, and, finally, 4) the continued recognition of one's need for deliverance from hidden fears, repressed conflicts, thwarted behavior, and impulsivity. Insofar as redeemers serve as channels of reclamation, they fulfill a legitimate role in religion. However, wherever redemption fails to achieve man's reclamation but results instead in self-righteousness, intolerance, arrogance, violence, and the repression of others, it cannot claim impunity from philosophical criticism. Why? Because humanity's greatest gift remains our capacity to transcend ourselves, to imagine a more honorable world in which to strive and live, and in which to fulfill our hopes and be transformed, as well as enjoy the fruits of reciprocity, such as love, justice, forgiveness, and harmony.

For many religions, this challenge has resulted in a slow transition. In the case of Hinduism, centuries were required. Slowly India witnessed the transition from its nomadic Aryan invasion—with its emphasis on animal sacrifice—to the era of the inner teachings of its rishis and gurus. Even the latter passed through periods of spiritual phases, beginning with the collected verses of the Vedas to the commentaries of the *Upanishads*, and from the *Upanishads* to the *Bhagavad Gita*. The latter remains of special interest, insofar as it preserves Hinduism's four cardinal paths of achieving "salvation." They are 1) the path of meditation, 2) submersion in the knowledge and study of God, 3) the way of good works, and 4) and the path of single-minded devotion in the form of *bhakti* or love. All are perceived as methods of reclamation, blessed by none other than Vishnu himself, who represents the personal manifestation of the mystery of Brahman. Whoever serves God with single-minded devotion, in any of these capacities, without thought of self-gain, attains to unity with the godhead and freedom from the endless cycles of rebirth.

Among Theravada Buddhists, only the individual can reclaim himself or herself. Only he or she alone can wake up and see the world as it is. No one can do that for a follower. Nonetheless, just as the Buddha awakened to the truth about suffering, realized what caused it, and pursued his method of the ego's self-extinction, so can anyone else. That path to salvation begins with the renunciation of one's ego as a separate entity, independent of other sentient beings, along with the acceptance of one's ontological impermanence, thereby extinguishing fear of the threat of nonbeing. Though the Buddha may not function in the life of a *bikkhus* as a forgiving Jesus, nonetheless, the Buddha's exemplary life, devotion to his followers, and establishment of the *sangha* constitutes a "redemptive" path for all. The Buddhist's chant of the Three Refuges, i.e., "I take refuge in the Buddha, I take refuge in the *Dhamma* (his teachings), I take refuge in the *sangha* (the community)" clearly witness to the Buddha's original dynamic role.

It is only in Christianity that the transition from God the Enemy to God the Companion remains problematic. The cross and resurrection constitute its central dogmas. Both incorporate elements of primitive religion and the classical era's quest for immortality. The two became wed in the aftermath of the historical Jesus' life and death. The Second Temple's emphasis on sacrifice and ritual, along with the Greco-Roman world's quest for immortality, united in the teachings of Paul to create the Christian faith that exists today. One cannot imagine that God—as mankind's source of inspiration, energy, and determination—could have had any part in requiring the passion and death of Jesus as an expiation of human pride, let alone of neglect of God. Such a dogma makes sense only when viewed as the history of man's recognition of his own alienation and failure to surmount himself. It is this man, historically, who, upon realizing how far short of his potential he had fallen and how desperate his need for redemption had become, who constructed the punitive means of his salvation. To that extent the cross represents mankind's own crucifixion for all that man has lost and for which he craves restitution; while the resurrection symbolizes his rectification to a new life. Metaphorically, these elements lie behind Pauline grace, which cannot be earned, and which, in Paul's view, flows from the compensatory activity of God's Son. It took John to venture the next step, in which he envisions God as the essence of love and Christ as the exemplar of God's forgiving nature. We cannot fault Paul for his time and place in history. Nor does Christianity need to divest itself of the cross and resurrection. Its challenge is to reinterpret both as redemptive means by which mankind achieves his reclamation as a self-determining human being whose life is best fulfilled when subservient to divine grace and love.

One might quarrel that the above compromises the value of "forgiveness of sin." However, neither the devaluing of forgiveness nor sin necessarily follows. Forgiveness is a cathartic and therapeutic means by which human beings seek reconciliation for themselves and one another, due to regrettable actions and words that have resulted in guilt and harm. Forgiveness makes possible the condition of grace, which allows persons to overcome hurt and remorse (over sin) and move forward with their lives. Not to forgive is as detrimental to the offended as to the offending party. Both stand in need of reconciliation. Jesus' post-Easter meeting with his eleven disciples illustrates this reality with profound psychological depth. "If you forgive the sins of any, they are forgiven; if you retain the sins of any they are retained" (John 20:23). Jesus knew that such forgiveness requires the Spirit of love. In keeping with YHWH's creation of the first man from the dust of the earth, John reports that Jesus "breathed" his Spirit upon his disciples, thus creating a new wave of human existence that Easter evening.

That God should be viewed as the ultimate Forgiver is also retainable. Without a sense of eternal grace, humans falter in their quest to fulfill their individual destinies. As the Spirit of the Ground of Being, who indwells and inspires all humankind, forgiveness and divine mercy go hand in hand in enabling persons to aspire to the highest level of self-attainment they are capable of achieving.

CHAPTER 12

The Light that Enlightens Everyone

RELIGIONS EAST AND WEST, Occidental and Asian, have all sought Enlightenment. A "God of the gaps" may have appealed to mankind's earlier religious quests, but today such an identification of God with "the gaps" attracts little more than embarrassment. As discussed throughout our text, no one can prove the existence of God. Yet it is difficult to eliminate the question of God, as the question is implicit in the mystery of the human condition. In part it is due to the human quest for knowledge, for our unbounded desire and unending curiosity to know the truth about ourselves and our universe. Though our immediate awareness of the possibility of God in no way proves God's existence, the question still remains inescapable. Granted, belief based on proofs is a mediated belief and not a belief "at first hand," man still hungers to know what to believe. Even knowing that the will to believe can never substitute for that Kierkegaardian "Moment" that calls us to believe, we still thirst for the truth. It is all part of the human longing to transcend deception and be grasped by the cognitive hand of truth and reality. Abraham symbolizes the quest in his own quiescent pilgrimage, as he risked the loss of his one and only son, his beloved and cherished son, Isaac, as he raised his knife in obedience to the call of the Absolute. One needs to remember that there is a valid, philosophical distinction between a "God of the gaps" and a "God of the depths." The first refers to the pre-scientific era's quest for explanations that its civilizations could not provide. The latter is in reference to the mystery of the human condition and its capacity of transcendence, its innate sense that God is at hand. No amount of scientific or empirical information can assuage humankind's search for that ultimate enlightening factor, apart from one's leap of faith, whether for or against the idea of God or its Eastern counterpart, Brahman.

Somewhere in Bultmann's writings he answers the question concerning that enlightening factor. It came to me "second hand," long ago, while devoting a year of life among brothers in a monastic équipe near Paris. The name of the Order was: Villémêtrie. Its director was André de Robert, a pastor of the Reformed Church of France and an admirer of Rudolf Bultmann's system of the demythologization of the New Testament. André's library contained a stack of French translations of the German's works. I was young, on leave from an American seminary, anguished of heart and drowning in my "skeptical doubt." As a student of philosophy, I was wed to Plato and Aristotle, Hume and Camus, as well as to a healthy hunk of Nietzsche, Albert Schweitzer, and Kierkegaardian literature. Also, as a lover of science and biology, I was thoroughly committed to the theory of evolution. I had no problem with a metaphorical or mythical evaluation of the Adamic story, then or now. But I was sick with despair, for how could I become a minister, knowing how little of the Christian credo I at that time could accept?

It was André's custom to meet with each brother once a month, just to chat and explore a brother's spiritual journey. When it came my time, late in the stay, he called me to his office. I sat near his desk; he sat across from me. With a kindness so few can ever evince, he asked: "*Mon frère*, what has truly brought you to Villémêtrie? You seem so troubled. I should love to know." After several moments of silence, I replied: "My doubt! I carry it everywhere I go. Wherever I am, it is there, deep inside me, everyday, all the time." He studied my face and countenance, smiled; then replied. "*Alors, mon cher*, do you remember what Paul says in 1 Cor 12:9? Faith is a gift. It is a gift of the Spirit." He paused and smiled again. "God never leaves any of us giftless, even when we think we have been left out. Think of it this way, God *has* given you a gift, but it is the *gift of doubt*." Later that year I asked him, "André, what do you really believe about God?" He thought for a moment, then replied: "'*Dieu est la manifestation du mystère de la condition humaine.*' I read that in Bultmann somewhere and have never ceased to believe it."

Bultmann's definition of God as "the manifestation of the mystery of the human condition" carries an appeal that holds its own against man's ordinary presuppositions in his search of understanding. Like Tillich's

Ground of Being, it is rooted in the human depths. It is part of the phenomenology of humanity. It is where all faith begins, whether in Yeats' "foul and rag-bone shop of the heart," or in the unassailable ontological precondition of human existence as it surfaces in the form of "existential doubt." *That is a reality*. That precondition exists. It does not "prove" God's existence in any sense. Nonetheless, the precondition of mankind's depths "proves" something about us—that we are aware of an unconditional element *within* ourselves that compels us to look *beyond* ourselves for self-fulfillment and enlightenment. That Hinduism answers it in terms of "Brahman," Buddhism in terms of "waking up," Islam in terms of Allah, or Zen in terms of the enlightenment experience itself, does not detract from its power to inspire humankind to look beyond the self for life's fullest enlightenment. This is not to say that the experience of the immanence of God within the self is invalid or without worth. Far from it, as such a tenet would invalidate the ennobling experiences of Eastern Religion as well as Christian mysticism. No. But it is said to affirm all that Hartshorne has so wisely encapsulated under his term "dual transcendence." Even the skeptical scientists' love of the universe witnesses to the reality of the human condition that longs for self-understanding, while nurtured by the galactic wonder of a trillion stars that telescopes track.

God may not exist in the way that human beings want God to exist, even in Dawkins' case. But as a metaphor of the inescapable precondition of mankind's existentiality and quest for understanding, belief in God unifies one's soul, mind, and spirit at a profound enlightening and therapeutic depth. The cruel excesses of religion have nothing to do with God, no more than the so-called "wrathful YHWH" of the Old Testament, or the bloodthirsty mullahs of Jihad. That religious cruelty exists in no way devalues the highest satisfaction to which religion can attain—that enlightenment that leads to God the Companion.

At a minimum, God exists as this metaphor, as life's transcendent and immanent reality that underlies the splendor and miracle of life. God's glory is seen in the sunrise and sunset, as Earth's orb turns on its axis to face its solar star, the Sun, everyday. In Hartshorne's view, we are the conscious extensions of this *immanent* phenomenon of *transcendent existentiality* we call God, if not a cellular shard of God's inimitable existence and power. Greek mythology, Judaism, Christianity, Kabbalism, and Hindu thought (i.e., its god Agni), have all identified God with light and life, or light and enlightenment, at one time or other. Indeed, fire has often served as the principal metaphor for God and God's gift of enlightenment. That early mankind worshiped fire is hardly an anomaly. For fire sustains and illuminates all, and leads from the shadows of Plato's cave to the glory of Light itself.

We may well have moved beyond the fire gods of Hawaii and the Andes, but ancient Greece's respect for Hephaistos is worth recalling.[1] According to various sources, he was a non-Greek by name. Originally, he hailed from the city of Hephaistias on the Island of Lemnos. Celebrated as the god of fire and blacksmiths, fresh fire from his altar was distributed to the city's craftsmen at an annual festival in his honor.

Legend has it that Hephaistias' citizens cared for Hephaistos after his mother Hera cast him from heaven. His long fall resulted in crushed ankles, crippling him for the rest of his immortality. Considered a second-class deity by most Greek cities, Athena favored him, and, thanks to her, a temple was erected in his tribute near the Acropolis. As god of fire, Hera later called on him to save her beloved Achilles when the latter was about to be drowned by the river god Skamandoros. Hephaistos was also associated with the natural gas fires that still burn along the coastline near Olympus.

The Olympian gods frequently snickered behind his back, since his wife Aphrodite was known to be carrying on an affair with Ares, the god of war. Nonetheless, even the gods had to admire his skill with metal and fire. He is especially remembered for his creation of a magnificent shield that depicted the entire world, framed by the dome of heaven above it. All in all, there is much to like about this god of fire, whose gift of heat and flame enabled the Greeks to fashion a plethora of useful goods. Nevertheless, this crippled god of the glowing embers was destined to remain a distant second to the Sun-god, Apollo, whose blazing light and illuminating rays brought life and light to the Greek mind, while assuaging its restive soul.

Upon reflection, the symbolism of fire and light is as pertinent today as it was for the Greeks. What we know of quantum physics and its understanding of electromagnetism leads us to wonder if God is not mirrored in that emanating fireball, both *within* and *behind* the universe's spontaneous creation. This is not a "God of the gaps," for there is no gap between the human condition and God as the Ground of Being. "Before Abraham was, I am," stated Jesus, or so the Evangelist John interpreted Jesus' existence to mean. "The kingdom of God is within you," Jesus added. "You are the light of the world." God is in you, as Krishna reminded Arjuna as he stood beside

---

1. See Burkert, *Greek Religion*, 167–68. The segment on Hephaistos above follows Burkert's discussion.

him on the back of his chariot. God is not some distant reality, unknowable and disassociated from the universe. The expanding universe itself mirrors God's immanence in every particle, in its waves, atoms, energy, electrons, elements, and memes that make both "stuff" and sentience possible. Reason requires the mind to posit God as transcendent, else God's subjection to entropy as atoms "die" makes God susceptible to diminution and decay. If this interpretation is true, God is within us; we are an extension of God's reality and will, both cognitively and physically, clothed in garments of whirling atoms and DNA. God's presence is mirrored in the fire and the light in the glowing electromagnetic field that makes possible human existence and sustains it throughout life, while undying and transcending mankind's mortal coil. Yes, this is metaphor, for metaphor is as much the language of reality as mathematics is the language of "stuff." This is why the physicist Alfred North Whitehead refused to settle for "God the Void," choosing instead to embrace "God the Companion."

God, by any other name, remains God: the totality of all that brings hope, enlightenment, and promise. God is the living beacon that inspires mankind to crave freedom and seek novelty in all we think and do. As has been explained earlier, the Greeks in their longing for meaning captured the same in their myths of Apollo and Dionysus. Both were sons of God, the one the symbol of enlightenment and restraint; the other the symbol of life's drunken pulse and intoxicating adventure. Both symbolized the essence of life, as Nietzsche so clearly perceived in his time. So too in the case of Moses, who experienced his own moment of enlightenment, standing shocked before the fiery "burning bush." Like Abraham of old, the "Moment" awakened him out of his nomadic slumbers, empowering him to see that the inherited gods (El, El Olam, El-Shaddai, and Elohim) of his Near Eastern ancestors were but wavering shadows of life's greatest light: "I am that I am." Humbled and shoeless, he bowed before that glorious apparition and rose enlightened to challenge the greatest powers of his day, becoming the Father of no less than three world religions: Judaism, Christianity, and Islam.

In this regard, one ought keep in mind Israel's own ancient and larger encounter with the God of fire. It is this God who guides the Israelites to the Promised Land in "his" column of cloud by day and pillar of fire by night, and, equally, by "his" holy righteous flames purges Israel from its sins and apostasy. It is this God who captures the imagination of Moses in the mystical bush as well as in "his" descent in the crackling blaze on Elijah's altar to reveal "his" presence as Israel's sole, one and only LORD.

In Hinduism, it is the god Agni, the god of fire, who comes to mind. For it is he who bears to heaven on the wings of Savitar's rays and Dawn's shimmering glow the hope and gratitude of mankind's dreams for each new day.

God is the metaphor of the *reality*, not just the mystery, of anything at all—the universe, as well as our consciousness of truth, beauty, and love. To know truth, beauty, and love, is to know God. Every hunger for enlightenment is a hunger for God, every insight of truth a gift from God, every response and experience of love a response and encounter with God, who is love (1 John 4:7, 16). For this reason God transcends all human notions of good and evil that justify cruelty, violence, and hate.

God as companion both stands at the door and opens the door into every now and tomorrow. Truth, goodness, and love are as precious handmaidens to religion as methodological doubt, math, and chemistry are to the language of science. The two are not oppositional ways to enlightenment and joy, but complementary paths to fathoming the depths of human existence, while exploring the splendor of humankind's star-bright universe.

As a student of philosophy and religion for most of my life, I have never discounted the value of Aquinas' much-maligned argument from necessity. That anything contingent exists requires a prior cause to account for its existence. If that cause itself is contingent, then it too requires a cause. The only way to stop this causal chain going on ad infinitum is for a cause to exist that transcends the linear scale of cause and effect, a phenomenon that exists in and of itself, of necessity. As engaging as the theory of "spontaneous creation" is, even a spontaneous eruption requires a mass, a phenomenon of "stuff," as well as time and space in order for it to ignite, and a mind that can grasp and express this concept for itself and other minds. Even the recent findings of the scientists seeking to substantiate the so-called Higgs boson, at best can only break it down into tinier sub-atomic particles or electro-magnetic fields. I see no way that the argument from necessity can ever be eliminated as a handmaiden of truth. At least, philosophically, it exists as a haunting residue of mankind's search for a wholeness that transcends the universe of mere "stuff." To define man in terms of an electro-magnetic field alone can never do justice to his quest for the meaning of his own grandeur and love of life. In some respects, his situation is a converse of the psalmist's question in Psalm 8. Instead of "what is man that Thou art mindful of him?" man's question becomes: "What art Thou that *I* am mindful of *Thee?*"

Forty-three years ago I sat alone, frightened and in sorrow, as my wife lay recovering from childbirth in a Charlottesville hospital. She had given birth to our second son, our first having died on the day he was born from "Hyland Membrane" as it was then called. Our second son, too, was born prematurely, with all the uncertainty associated with survival. I had left my wife pale and in shock in the hospital, as together our eyes betrayed our fear of a second loss. That night, at home, while I sat in the kitchen of our manse, I bowed my head and cried. I wept for my wife, as well as myself, and for all the dreams we had savored as becoming parents. Slowly, I struggled to gather myself together in an attempt to accept reality as it was. With a sadness as deep as the sea, I put my hands to my face and prayed: "Dear God, please remember us in this hour of waiting. And grant, O God, my wife the courage and love to accept whatever happens." As a lover of truth and reality, I had done all I knew to do. It was my moment on Mt. Moriah. Then, without realizing what was happening, I felt myself moving suddenly away from my body. It was quite abrupt. I could feel it, as if I were being lifted up, and rather quickly at that. What is this? My mind objected. What's going on here? My face was still wet with tears, then suddenly a brilliant emanation—more glorious than any light I have ever seen—encompassed me and filled me with inexplicable peace. It seemed to engulf me out of nowhere, as if the heavens had opened for all its light to slip through. Never had I known such calm, then or since. The moment lasted only briefly—hardly as long as Eben's disabled cortex vibrated with wonder of its own—but I knew instinctively that *that than which none greater can be experienced* had lifted me into its presence. The next morning I rushed to the hospital and tore up the steps to the third or forth floor to the neonatal ward where our son had been placed in a tiny englassed oxygen unit. A nurse saw me at the window, smiled, reached into his little tent, and brought him to the window. So tiny he was, but alive and breathing. Then I hurried to my wife's room to report the good news.

I have never told this story before, nor do I want to again. After all, as André explained, my gift of the Spirit was *doubt*. And, as I reflect on it, life's Giver gave me a hefty measure at that. So too, it is likely that one day the paranormal, out-of-body experiences, and the gene that prepares life for its sorrows and shocks, will be stretched out and etherized upon the table of modern science and fully understood. Yet, the luminous wonder that embraced me that night was as ontologically intense as my despair and sorrow.

"God is light, and in him is no darkness at all" (1 John 1:5). Why anyone would want to destroy that Light, even if only a metaphor, is beyond comprehension. Shy of a postscript, Alfred North Whitehead still captured it best: "Religion is . . . , if it evolves to its final satisfaction, . . . the transition from God the void to God the enemy, and from God the enemy to God the companion."[2]

---

2. Whitehead, *Religion in the Making*, 16.

CHAPTER 13

The Hiddenness of God

No study of the philosophy of religion would be complete without examining Martin Buber's reference to the hiddenness of God. Hailed as "the greatest living Jewish philosopher"[1] of the past century, his book *Eclipse of God* still stands as a masterpiece of reflection on the relation between philosophy and religion. While appreciative of aspects of Martin Heidegger's existentialism and a beneficiary of Søren Kierkegaard's anti-Hegelian stance, he criticized each and, in the same vein, put Sartre's views to the test. What disenchanted Buber was both Heidegger and Sartre's starting point: Nietzsche's "the death of God."

Heidegger's emphasis on "dwelling" especially evoked Buber's concern. As many readers know, Heidegger's philosophical system draws much of its inspiration from elements of Friedrich Hölderlin's poetry. For the latter, the whole task of the poet and his counterpart, the philosopher, is to accept the "default" of God as a fact of history. The hero gods of the past are gone. They will not be coming back. Thus the poet's task is to sing the wine god Dionysus' song, while mankind's task is to pick up the pieces and search the sky for a new "god," or metaphysical reality. Heidegger discusses this search at length in his *Sein und Zeit*, as well as in *Poetry, Language, Thought*. Note the sequence: that poetry appears first, then language, and finally thought. It is the language of the poet that expresses one's existential condition and opens the way to self-understanding. Until the metaphysician can establish

---

1. Reinhold Niebuhr's comment on the dust jacket of *Eclipse of God*.

a new world order, however, the poet's task is clear: to inspire and salvage the human condition.

The most captivating verses of Hölderlin's poems suggest that humanity cannot help but live poetically upon the earth, in the light of the default of the hero gods. Heidegger made this central to his philosophical system. What disturbed Buber was Heidegger's willingness to dispense with the biblical God of Western metaphysics, without genuine qualms, simply taking Nietzsche's "death of God" and Hölderlin's views as his starting point. For Buber, such a ploy removed God "from the realm of objective being to the 'imminence of subjectivity.'"[2] Even more, it underscored modern thought and its inability to "endure a God who is not confined to man's subjectivity."[3] Simply to know God in "one's self-encounters with the self" is insufficient. Buber praised Heidegger for recognizing that the slaying of God meant "the elimination of the self-subsisting suprasensual world." However, that was not the crucial point:

> [For] the living God who approaches and addresses an individual in the situation of real life is not a component part of such a suprasensual world; His place is no more there than it is in the sensible world, and, whenever man nonetheless has to interpret encounters with Him as self-encounters, man's very structure is destroyed.[4]

> To-day, when we are faced by the question of our destiny, the question as to the essential difference between all subjectivity and that which transcends it [is misleading] without man's again experiencing and accepting his real encounters with the divine as such.[5]

In concluding his criticism of Heidegger, Buber appealed to his own concept of the Eternal "Thou" to recapture the religious sense of God as man's true *vis-à-vis*. Tying this in with the title of his book, he reiterated his view that only an encounter with the God who transcends man's subjectivity can enable one to overcome "the human responsibility for the eclipse" of God.[6] Even if the world did away with the name of God, God as man's *vis-à-vis* would live intact, for, "He who is denoted by the name lives in

---

2. Ibid., 21.
3. Ibid.
4. Ibid., 22.
5. Ibid., 23.
6. Ibid., 24.

the light of His eternity. But we, 'the slayers,' remain dwellers in darkness, consigned to death."[7]

In clarifying what he meant by "encounter," Buber stated:

> The personal manifestation of the divine is not decisive for the genuineness of religion. What is decisive is that I relate myself to the divine as to Being which is over against me, though *not* over against me *alone*. . . . It is not necessary to know something about God in order to believe in Him; many true believers know how to talk *to* God but not *about* Him. If one dares to turn toward the unknown God, to go to meet Him, to call to Him, Reality is present. He who refuses to limit God to the transcendent has a fuller conception of Him than he who does so limit Him. But he who confines God within the immanent means something other than Him.[8]

What Buber wished to confirm was that God is beyond both objectivity and subjectivity. God encounters us in the mystery of our existence much as Tillich's Ground of Being encounters us in the inescapable "depths" of our existence and in the "existential doubt" of all our days. As such, God comes to us in and on God's own terms, as neither a component of the suprasensual world or as a phenomenon of the sensible world of stuff. Buber's rootage in the deep mysticism of his Judaism shines through his analyzes at every turn.

Similarly, Buber was critical of Sartre, whose departure point was also Nietzsche's *"Dieu n'existe pas."* What especially annoyed Buber was Sartre's statement in his essay *Existentialism* in which Sartre writes: "[God] is dead, . . . he spoke to us and now is silent, all that we touch now is his corpse."[9] Buber considered the latter part of this statement to be "shockingly trivial," but he was game to comment on its precedent, "he spoke to us and now is silent." What if that is true? asks Buber. What if it should mean precisely what the Hebrew Bible understands it to mean? That the living God is both a "self-revealing but also a self-concealing God?" And what does that mean for us who "live in the age of such a concealment, such a divine silence?" What "part of our not hearing and our not having heard has played [a role] in that silence"? Sartre's argument that the only universe is a universe of human subjectivity is a rejection of the living God who meets us as life's

7. Ibid.
8. Ibid., 28.
9. Ibid., 66.

only true Other, who is "the undefinable and unfathomable" absolute of the "reciprocal relation of I and Thou." That we become aware of God's silence in rejecting God points directly to mankind's "religious need" to know the Eternal God and to know God as no other.[10]

In a television interview (whose date I cannot remember), a journalist asked Richard Dawkins how he would react if upon his death he should meet God. Dawkins smiled and replied: "I would ask him why he hid from us and didn't want us to know him." Buber's analysis above provides the salient answer. Nonetheless, Dawkins' question is well taken, though hardly new. Throughout the Old Testament, the psalmists and prophets alike wrestled with God's silence, God's apparent withdrawal, or God's hiddenness when his nation needed him most. Time and again, the references are couched in the form of the phrase: "I shall hide my face from them" [in the Prophets], and "hide not thy face from me" [in the Psalms]. The first represents a *foundational awareness* of God's hiddenness while the second an *ontological awareness*. Passages in Isaiah, Jeremiah, Ezekiel, and Micah express YHWH's judgment against his people for having turned aside from that which constitutes God's *foundational* relationship with Israel: YHWH alone is God; there can be no other! The darkness, sorrow, and national woe that befalls them stands in consequence of Israel's "turning away." In fact, in Hebrew, the verb for turning away is *phanah*, while the noun for face is *pheni*. Because Israel has turned its face from God, it has brought upon itself its own default. God has been forced to withdraw from their idolatrous behavior and arrogant delusions. Why? Because these have nothing in common with the Eternal Other, from which the Israelites have separated themselves. Isaiah 8:17; 54:8; 59:2; Jer 33:5; Ezek 39:22–29; and Mic 3:4 highlight the silence of God's withdrawal from his people's world. Yet many of these passages express YHWH's desire to gather God's people unto God again.

> For a brief moment I abandoned you, but with great compassion I will gather you.
> In overflowing wrath for a moment I hid my face from you, but with everlasting love I will have compassion on you, says the Lord, your Redeemer. (Isa 54:7–8)

The references in the psalms fall into two categories or modes, both of which preserve elements of humankind's ontological condition. The word

---

10. Ibid., 67–68.

THE HIDDENNESS OF GOD

"mode" is preferred over "category," as "mode" best preserves the exigencies of life. The primary mode is *remorse,* or regret. It arises in the form of the recognition of God's deserved concealment and silence because of Israel's guilt. It is primary inasmuch as it leaves the Israelite without recourse. The other mode is *dread*, or that "sickness unto death," as Kierkegaard labeled it, that witnesses to the depths of existence with all the uncertainty that characterizes thought and action. We find the first modeled in the following:

> As for me, I said in my prosperity, "I shall never be moved."
> By your favor, O Lord, . . . you hid your face; [and] I was dismayed. (Ps 30:8)

The second mode is equally prevalent. It occurs as the acknowledgment of man's uncertainty, his hidden anxiety and fear that precede every thought and act. For it is in these moments that man faces the Absoluteness of God, whether as the abyss, the depths, the enemy in one's own mirror, or as one's hope and promise of fulfillment.

Psalm 88 contains a prime example of such dread:

> O Lord, why do you cast me off? Why do you hide your face from me?
> I suffer your terrors; I am desperate.
> Your wrath has swept over me, your dread assaults destroy me.

Or again in Ps 143: 7:

> Answer me quickly, O Lord, my spirit fails.
> Do not hide your face from me, or I shall be like those who go down to the Pit.

Yet even here, this encounter of the self with its failing spirit, draws one only closer to the hidden God. As the psalmist continues: "Let me hear of your steadfast love in the morning, for in you I put my trust" (v. 8).

Even faith, however, is no guarantee that all "fear and trembling" will be eliminated. Even in moments of faith, the Israelite experienced the absence of God. It is that dark side of faith that tests man to the core.

> Because of you we are being killed all day long, and accounted as sheep for the slaughter.
> Rouse yourself! Why do you sleep, O Lord? Awake, do not cast us off forever!
> Why do you hide your face? Why do you forget our affliction and oppression? (Ps 44:22–24)

In part, for this reason, Buber warns not to proceed too quickly down the path of Whitehead's transitions. As Buber explains:

> He who begins with the love of God without having previously experienced the fear of God, loves an idol which he himself has made, a god whom it is easy enough to love. He does not love the real God who is, to begin with, dreadful and incomprehensible. Consequently, if he then perceives, as Job and Ivan Karamazov perceive, that God is dreadful and incomprehensible, he is terrified. He despairs of God and the world if God does not take pity on him, as He did on Job, and bring him to love Him Himself. . . . That the believing man who goes through the gate of dread is directed to the concrete contextual situations of his existence means just this: that he endures in the face of God the reality of lived life, dreadful and incomprehensible though it be. He loves it in the love of God, whom he has learned to love.[11]

And so we return to the opening questions of chapter 1: "does God exist?" Or, "does it even matter that God exists?" The believer who answers "Yes" may well carry his or her moments of doubt till the hour of death, but as Hartshorne has tried to demonstrate, that person will never cease to be, at least, as a "cell" in God's eternal existence. Indeed, even the skeptic's memory will endure beside the believer's in the reality of God's dual transcendence.

During the height of the Hasidic movement in Central Europe, Rabbi Kotzk surprised a group of learned visitors with the question: "Where is the dwelling of God?" "Why, what a thing to ask!" they laughed. "The whole world is full of his glory." But the rabbi knew how glib their answer was. "No," he replied: "God dwells wherever man lets him in."[12]

Two millennia ago wise men from the East followed a star to where it came to rest over a little town called Bethlehem. There they knelt to worship a child, wrapped in swaddling clothes and lying in a manger. Today's wise men also track stars, indeed, a host of them; where some have come to rest over the towns of Oxford, Cambridge, and Harvard. There, too, the wise men kneel in allegiance to the splendor of heaven. But the Star of Stars, before whom all Earth's wise men kneel, remains the same and sheds its light for all to see.

---

11. Ibid., 36–37.
12. Buber, *Tales of the Hasidim*, Book Two, 277.

CHAPTER 14

Magna Est Veritas: A Postscript

In moments of our greatest clarity, why is it that we humans pause to reflect on God at all? And why is it that some seek with fervor to eradicate the very question of God from humankind's thought? Either way, the question of God in unavoidable. It is inescapable, for it is grounded in the mystery of the self and underlies both mankind's conscious as well as subconscious moments.

One of the more engaging stories in the Apocryphal books of the Old Testament may be found in 1 Esdras. The story is set during the reign of Darius (521–485 BCE) and opens with three bodyguards deciding to write essays concerning the "strongest" of anything. It is their hope that the king will favor one of their essays and lavish the writer with unimaginable riches. The first wrote about *wine*; the second, the *king*, and the third, *women*. Playful, yet serious, each contender was permitted to present his essay before the king and his advisers.

The first bodyguard addressed the king with trembling enthusiasm. Contrasting and comparing the effects of *wine*, he listed its strengths along with its drawbacks. Yes, it clouds the mind, makes equals of kings and servants, slave and free, poor and rich, lifting mankind into mirth and joy, beyond his sorrows and mounting debts. Sometimes it results in quarrels and violence, but upon the sunrise of life's tomorrows, the quarrels fade away. What greater diversion and portal to happiness could one want?

The second bodyguard spoke on the value of *monarchy*, listing both its virtues and vices. Power, majesty, authority and dominion derive from a king. Victory and glory, as well as servitude and taxes flow from his royal throne. To obey is expected; to rebel ruinous. There is no greater power than his. For good or evil, kingship has no equal.

Finally, the third bodyguard steps forward—the fabled Zerubbabel. His topic: *women*. But only as a ruse, as something greater than women has drawn him to the podium. Nonetheless, his speech honors women as noble, as well as acknowledging the irreplaceable role women play in life. Indeed, "men cannot exist without women" (1 Esd 4:17). As his lover, childbearer, and caretaker to his last days, nothing exceeds her glory or beauty, value and merit throughout his life. Then, with something of an appeal to the king's lighter side, Zerubbabel teases Darius for the playful manner in which Apame, his favorite concubine, amuses and abuses him, as she takes off his crown and places it on her own head. All turn to smile at the king, then stare back. Now Zerubbabel has come to the moment of truth. He can no longer play the role of an innocent jester. The king must know the truth. Neither wine, nor the monarchy, nor women comprises man's highest hope, nor can lift man to life's highest satisfaction. Only truth, and the God of truth, can suffice. "*Magna est veritas et praevalet*," as the Clementine Vulgate reads. "Great is truth, and it prevails."

Of course, wine, the king, and women are reflective of far more profound longings than passing pleasure or the quest for fairness and equity. Wine denotes man's longing for immortality, such as the Greek god Dionysus could bestow; the king, the evasive symbol of man's hungering for peace and justice, prosperity and joy; while women represent mankind's longing for offspring and legacy, that is, for children to care for and to remember a man in his declining years. The three topics are tantamount to answers to Tillich's analysis of the human condition, which is filled with anxiety due to its awareness of the threat of nonbeing and meaninglessness. But in the end, neither wine, nor justice, nor women can fill the gap that God alone can satisfy, who remains life's highest good and greatest truth of all.

What both science and religion hunger to know, pursue, venerate, and value is the *truth*. In an ideal world, neither "field" need hate the other, nor deny the other's role to name the universe. Each is a means of our human self-exploration as we journey from eon to eon across the span of time. What is the purpose of the universe if God should not exist? It would have no purpose without a purpose giver. You and I are that purpose giver as we marvel at it all. You and I are the "I Am" that has come into consciousness to name, cherish, create, and preserve all that is best and brightest in behalf of all. The extent to which both science and religion unite to pursue that truth ennobles us, without either insisting that's its way *alone* knows the truth.

Some things are incommunicable. Such is the case, whether it is the truth that the mystical heart experiences as it soars upward in its journey of transcendence, or the marvel that the scientist feels as he/she sits at the telescope and beholds the glorious spectra of colors that glow in spirals of floating nebulae for the scientist to observe, photograph, number, and catalog.

APPENDIX A

Athens and Jerusalem

SINCE THE TIME OF Tertullian, the question has been asked repeatedly: "What has Athens to do with Jerusalem? What concord is there between the Academy and the church?"[1] It raises the age-old dilemma between faith and reason. For many contemporary scientific scholars and select persons come-of-age, reason does not require an intelligent Designer to account for the universe, nor a God mankind must believe in, praise, or worship, nor in any binding religious dogma or religious ethical system. The Renaissance and Enlightenment have long pushed mankind past such considerations. Nonetheless, the question remains, and, like Hegel's "Owl of Minerva," has taken wing and swooped down in its nightly hunt to trouble science and religion again.

In many respects Greek religion underlies the rise and development of Greece's wisest and most enduring philosophers. Homer and the Olympian gods visibly indwell the masterworks of the Greek playwrights and Plato's philosophy. This is especially so in the case of the latter's dismissal of the poets, due to their inability to grasp the higher ideals that bring order and justice to life. Nonetheless, Plato's highest Good, attainable by the ascent of reason, turns out to be the Olympian Zeus in all his better nature. The last book of the *Phaedrus* is sheer religious poetry, in which mankind race in their rickety chariots behind Zeus and his immortals' glowing chariots, as mankind panic to keep up with God. Once they take their eyes off of God, however, down they glide into that *katabolé*, that "fall," from whence the return to God requires up to 10,000 years—or so mulls Socrates in the

---

1. Tertullian, *Prescriptions Against Heretics*, ANF, 3:525. Cited by Gonzales, *History of Christian Thought*, 179.

APPENDIX A

Phaedrus. What Nietzsche maintains about Socrates and Plato's elevating Apollo over Dionysus echoes the Greek love of reason—though within the bounds of its beloved myths—inasmuch as Apollo's restraint was needed in order to make sense of life and apply appropriate brakes on mankind's intoxication with self-destructive passions. Thus, reason became a path to salvation, while not totally replacing the gods. *Nous* became the gateway to truth, inasmuch as reason was deemed superior to the lusts of the *sarx* and its debilitating bondage to concupiscence and libido. Stoicism and Epicureanism shared the same goal—theirs, too, being a leap of faith emboldened by reason.

Even the most casual student of philosophy today realizes Augustine's indebtedness to Platonic and Neoplatonic philosophy. His earliest essays abound with the Platonic intellectual steps necessary to ascend to the pure and unsullied mind of God; plus, his analyses of the city of God and the city of Man are derivatives of the benefits of Plato's intellectual realm vs. the sorrows of mankind's physical realm, mired in impermanence, ignorance, and decay. In this scenario, Athens had very much to do with Jerusalem. Without the former, Christianity could not have expressed its inspirational love of the Christ, nor fashioned the language requisite to secure his unique personage in history. A careful study of the rise of Buddhism reflects a similar history.

The same holds true for the ascent of theology throughout the early and late medieval periods of Western Society—from Anselm to Peter Abelard to Aquinas himself. Only with the rise of the Enlightenment, which Kant defined as "daring to think for one's self," did this bridge between Athens and Jerusalem begin to show signs of fatigue and stress. John Locke sought to rescue the union by finding faith reasonable and a perfect example of natural religion. That the universe should require a Creator, man redemption, and life strive for moral purpose appeared clearly in harmony with nature at its best. His product was entitled *The Reasonableness of Christianity.* Kant took the next step by subsuming faith completely under reason. His *Religion within the Limits of Reason Alone* promised a universal and fitting rationale for the role of religion, free from the subtitles of distinct religions and their idiosyncrasies. For this reason, Kant's God more closely mirrors Aristotle's abstract Unmoved Mover than the biblical God of Scriptures.

We live in the aftermath of this previously revered though debated union between faith and reason. Today it teeters once again on a wave of potential collapse, especially between science and religion. It is a facet of the cultural milieu of our time and marks a watershed similar to others from whence either faith falters or recovers, if not sometimes grows stronger. Even the Taoists find strength in Lao Tzu's knowledge that *faith* in the Tao is like water that transforms the mightiest rock into a smooth and beautiful stone. One thinks of Jesus' words: "And I tell you, you are Peter, and on this rock I will build my church, and the gates of death shall not prevail against it" (Matt 16:18). Religious people, as well as scientists and philosophers, historians and poets, who value this dialogue for its spiritual and existential inspiration, could not have their tasks assigned with greater clarity or urgency.

In the long run, faith requires reason in order to prevent it from sliding off the steep brink into superstition, anti-intellectualism, narcissistic spiritual self-indulgence, and irrelevance. So too reason limps up the hill of Nietzsche's "loneliest loneliness" and down through the valley of Tillich's angst of mankind's existential modes, unless a greater than ourselves fills that hollow remainder of endless quiet retreat. Even Eastern Buddhism, with its emphasis on meditation and mindfulness, requires the support of reason concerning its search for peace and harmony with its Ground of Being. To Hartshorne's credit, as well as that of Marcel and Heidegger's holy poets, singing their songs for God in a destitute time, he refused to surrender belief in God. So too Whitehead, though the latter defined God in intellectual and therapeutic ways necessary to jumpstart the present time. We should not misuse "faith" to undermine the ascent of "reason." Nor does "reason" need to disparage the consolation of religion in its healing, moral, and aesthetic form.

Matthew Arnold attempted to address the commonalities and disparities of this union in his analysis of Hellenism and Hebraism, the former a requisite for its logic, disimpassioned reason, and love of order, while the latter emphasized man's individual response to the Thou of the universe in terms of faith, compassion, and an equal love of order. Albert Camus offered his own demythologized version in his comparison of Nordic versus Mediterranean temperaments, the former similar to Arnold's Hellenist vistas, with the latter a mixture of Dionysian and Hebraic qualities.[2] Few have surmised the value of the two as relevantly as Walter Kaufmann in his *Critique of Religion and Philosophy*.

For Kaufmann, reason is inseparable from "man's profoundest passion, the aspiration to be as God." Reason provides necessary concepts and

2. See Camus, *Lyrical Essays*, 189–98.

universals, without which man's faith could not be monitored, or subjected to the truth of what is given and what constitutes being. Like faith, "reason can never be at home in this world. On the wings of searching questions, it transcends beliefs and facts and all that is." Far from being cold and dispassionate, reason incorporates a dimension of excitement and passion equal to anything science can produce. "Gods and Ideas are potent reminders of man's dissatisfactions with all that is given in this world." Reason can never stop with simple facts alone but must ever subject them to criticism. Its argument with religion occurs when the latter takes comfort in its blind dogmas and inadequate visions, making it sterile and irrelevant to today's needs. Nonetheless, even reason must honor the "aspiration which is the soul of religion."[3]

In the case of religion, Kaufmann defines the subject as "authoritarian poetry," a form of "mysticism and morality, loyalty and aspiration." It aims to transform human life. At its best, "religion kindles and cultivates man's dissatisfaction with himself and helps him to raise himself higher." But once it mistakes itself for science, "it deserves disparagement." In the end, it is "like man himself."[4]

Thus we return once again to the psalmist's enduring question, as well as our own: "What is man that thou art mindful of him?" (Ps 8:4a]) Or, "Who art Thou that we art mindful of Thee?"

---

3. See Kaufmann, *Critique*, 429–31.
4. Ibid., 368.

APPENDIX B

Karl Barth's Rejection of the *Analogia Entis*

ALTHOUGH BARTH HAS SCARCELY been mentioned in this book's critique, his fundamental positions regarding philosophy and religion deserve brief attention. In Barth's massive program of Dogmatic Theology, the church's task is to safeguard its unique dogma, thus precluding any allegiance to philosophical or epistemological grounds that traditional metaphysics has required. Barth's approach is entirely theological, his starting point being God's sundering encounter with a fallen mankind whose finest attempts to fathom God at the human level are destined to fail. God and man have nothing in common with any "analogy of being" that would support man's "intellectual ascent," or spiritual unity with God. There is no Ground of Being here that champions man's idea of God, nothing warranting any justification from a human or theological viewpoint. All fallen man's *ratio* can recognize is humanity's distance, separateness, and alienation from God and man's longing to be healed, which even God must awaken in him. God has to do it all, so to speak, in order to rescue and redeem this fallen creature. Moreover, the only grounds on which this possibility can occur rests on God's sole initiative. It is entirely reliant on God's terms alone, as revealed in the church's scriptures and in the life, death, and resurrection of God's Son, Jesus Christ. Thus the church's task is to create a theology that protects and promulgates this knowledge, which is beyond humanity and nowhere else available.

All this reads quite well, but it imposes remarkable restrictions on philosophy's need to critique a dogmatic system. For one thing, Barth's undertaking is purely theological, or an intricate and convoluted history of past patristic, medieval, Reformation, and orthodox views. Much of this history is retained, though criticized along the way. Barth's real starting point is his Trinitarian theology, which he reads back into the scriptures of the Old Testament. By doing so, Barth's system attempts to by-pass or nullify any metaphysical grounds of objection and redress. There can be none, as Barth's God is beyond the reach of human reason and its categories. In Whitehead's language, Barth presents us with a case of "extreme transcendence," disavowing any possibility of immanence except on God's terms. The same proves to be the case with respect to Barth's epistemological basis. It is a dogmatic delineation of "divine encounters" as preserved in God's "revealed Word" contained in the Old and New Testaments of the Christian scriptures. Unfortunately, Barth can offer no objective epistemological justification for choosing the Christian church's scriptures over other religions' sacred writings. But then he doesn't need to, as his subject is *Church Dogmatics*, not a study of salvation history, worldwide.

From a negative viewpoint, his system is simply and purely apodictic and dogmatic. It is a refined "in-house" theological discussion applicable primarily to those who share or reject his views. In that respect, it is a self-contained adventure, more concerned with differentiating itself from metaphysics and science, than providing phenomenological insight into our authentic existentiality. It places God adrift in a realm as esoteric as Plato's Zeus and cohort immortals chasing after the Good across a timeless dome of sky. Barth creates a reductionist dogma encapsulated in a world all his own. In turn, the latter is knowable only within the bounds of Christianity's Trinitarian views. His only justification rests on God's "extreme transcendence," which begs exposition, if there exists no *analogia entis* between God and man. For this reason, Tillich's more ontological approach sheds a brighter light on the philosophy of religion than Barth's dogmatic system.

From a positive side, Barth still has much to contribute. In many respects, he is closer to Buber than Augustine, Luther than Calvin, yet as knowledgeable of the human condition as Heidegger. Rightfully so, he shares Buber's concern for a theology of immanence that fails to acknowledge the sinful consequences of fallen man. The religious realm of "inwardness" cannot substitute for an authentic encounter with the God of the patriarchs and the biblical prophets, let alone the evangelists' Gospels of Christ's cross and resurrection. For this reason, Barth rejects any knowledge of God from within. He was critical of Augustine's inward Platonic ascent to the divine Wholly Other God. Consequently, he labeled Augustine's "inwardness" a misleading attempt to find God. That is not how God reveals himself. Man plays no role in God's self-revelation. There is no analogy of being that supports man's cooperation with God. As he explains in *The Word of God and the Word of Man*, "The Bible tells us not how we should talk with God but what he says to us; not how we find the way to him but how he has sought and found the way to us."[1]

Nonetheless, Barth attempted to soften his emphasis on God's extreme transcendence by defining God as one who "exists" for man, whom he has loved and brought into being from the depths of his grace before the foundations of the earth were laid. As such, "the God of the Gospel is no lonely God, self-sufficient and self-contained." He has no equal, to be sure, but he is "not imprisoned by his own majesty." He chooses to be "the God of *man*." Moreover, "He is man's God not only as Lord but also as father, brother, friend," which displays a confirmation of God's very essence as distinct from man while being for man.[2]

All in all, however, it is clear that Barth favors God's transcendence. Any immanence is by God's Word alone, not a phenomenological sense of God's inwardness, which lifts one's spirit into the calm of mystical union with God. That numerous religious persons of all religions should favor a God of immanence over an abstract God of transcendence is understandable, as the former fills the supplicant with a dynamic, numinous feeling of God's *presence than which none closer can be experienced*. Here the religious person comes to his or her moment of truth, face to face with religion's paradoxical demand: linked to God by life's *analogia entis*, yet humbled and subdued by his knowledge of his human condition. The choice has never been between the two but one that embraces the two. Otherwise, God cannot be known, nor man realize his true self-fulfilment.

---

1. Barth, *Word of God*, 43.
2. Barth, *Evangelical Theology*, 11.

Selected Bibliography

Abernethy, George, and Thomas Langford. *History Of Philosophy*. Belmont, CA: Dickenson, 1967.
Alexander, Eben. "Heaven is Real." *Newsweek*, October 15, 2012.
Anselm. *The Major Works*. Oxford: Oxford University Press, 1998.
———. *Proslogion*. In *Anselm of Canterbury*. Oxford: Oxford University Press, 2008.
Aquinas, Thomas. *Summa Contra Gentiles* I. South Bend, IN: Notre Dame University Press, 1975.
Aristotle. *Basic Writings of Aristotle*. New York: Random House, 1971.
Barth, Karl. *Church Dogmatics* Vol. I. Part 1. Translated and edited by G. W. Bromiley. Edinburgh: T. & T. Clark, 1975.
———. *Evangelical Theology: An Introduction*. New York: Holt, Rinehart, Winston, 1963.
———. *The Word of God and the Word of Man*. New York: Harper & Brothers, 1957.
Borg, Marcus. *Meeting Jesus Again for the First Time*. San Francisco: Harper, 1994.
Buber, Martin. *Eclipse of God*. New York: Harper Torchbooks, 1952.
———. *Tales of the Hasidim*, 1–2. Translated by Olga Marx. New York: Schocken. 1991.
Burkert, Walter. *Greek Religion*. Cambridge: Harvard University Press, 1977.
Camus, Albert. *Lyrical and Critical Essays*. Translated by Ellen Kennedy. New York: Vintage, 1970.
Copleston, Frederik, and Bertrand Russell, "Third Programme of the British Broadcasting Corporation." In *Classical and Contemporary Readings in the Philosophy of Religion*, edited by John Hick, 226–44. Englewood Cliffs, NJ: Prentice Hall, 1990.
Dalai Lama. *Freedom in Exile*. New York: Harper Collins, 1990.
Dawkins, Richard. *The God Delusion*. Boston: Mariner, 2008.
Dionysus the Areopagite. *Complete Works of Dionysus*. Translated by Paul Rorem et al. New York: Oxford University Press, 1988.
Feuerbach, Ludwig. *The Essence of Christianity*. Translated by George Eliot. London: Chapman, 1854.
Gonzales, Justo. *A History of Christian Thought*, Vol. 1. Nashville: Abingdon, 1970.
Hardy, Thomas. "The Oxen." In *British Literature: From Blake to the Present Day*, edited by Hazelton Spenser, Walter Houghton, and Herbert Barrows, 837. Boston: Heath, 1952.
Hartshorne, Charles. *Omnipotence and Other Theological Mistakes*. Albany, NY: The University of New York Press, 1984.

SELECTED BIBLIOGRAPHY

Hawking, Stephen. *The Grand Design*. New York: Bantam, 2010.
Heidegger, Martin. *Poetry, Language, Thought*. Translated by A. Hofstadter. New York: Perennial Classics, 2001.
Hick, John, ed. *Classical and Contemporary Readings in the Philosophy of Religion*. 3rd ed. Englewood Cliffs, NJ: Prentice Hall, 1990.
Hume, David. *An Inquiry Concerning Human Understanding*, Section X. In *Classical and Contemporary Readings in the Philosophy of Religion*, 3rd ed., edited by John Hick, 107–20. Englewood Cliffs, NJ: Prentice Hall, 1990.
Humphries, Christian. *Buddhism*. London: Penguin, 1972.
James, William. *The Variety of Religious Experience*. New York: Collier, 1961.
Jones, W. T. *A History of Western Philosophy*. New York: Harcourt, Brace, 1952.
Kant, Emmanuel. *Critique of Pure Reason*. In *The European Philosophers from Descartes to Nietzsche*, edited by Monroe Beardsley, 375–98. New York: Modern Library, 1960.
Kaufmann, Walter. *Critique of Religion and Philosophy*. 1958. Reprint. Princeton: Princeton University Press, 1990.
Kierkegaard, Søren. *Fear and Trembling*. Garden City, NY: Doubleday Anchor, 1954.
———. *Philosophical Fragments or a Fragment of Philosophy*. Translated by Howard V. Hong. Princeton: Princeton University Press, 1971.
Lao Tzu. *Tao Te Ching*. London: Penguin Classics, 1963.
Luther, Martin. *Luther's Works, Vol. 14. Selected Psalms III*. Saint Louis: Concordia, 1958.
Neihardt, John. *Black Elk Speaks*. Lincoln, NE: University of Nebraska Press, 1988.
Nietzsche, Friedrich. *The Birth of Tragedy*. Translated by Walter Kaufmann. New York: Vintage, 1967.
———. *The Gay Science*. Translated by W. Kaufmann. New York: Vintage, 1974.
———. *On the Genealogy of Morals*. Translated by W. Kaufmann. New York: Vintage, 1969.
Philo of Alexandria. *De Officio Mundi*. Loeb Classics Library. Cambridge: Harvard University Press, 1971.
Plato. *Timaeus*. In *The Dialogues of Plato*, Vol. 2, translated by B. Jowett, 3–68. New York: Random House, 1937.
Plotinus. *Enneads*, I. Cambridge: Harvard University Press, 1978.
Randall, John. *Role of Knowledge in Western Religion*. Boston: Beacon, 1958.
Ricoeur, Paul. *The Symbolism of Evil*. Translated by E. Buchanan. Boston: Beacon, 1969.
Rig Veda—Sacred Writings of Hinduism. Translated by T. H. Griffiths. New York: Quality Paperback Book Club, 1992.
Russell, Bertrand. *Why I Am Not a Christian*. New York: Touchstone, 1957.
Sangharakshita. *The Three Jewels*. New York: Anchor, 1970.
Sartre, Jean Paul. "Existentialism is a Humanism." In *The Fabric of Existentialism*, edited by Richard Gill and Ernest Sherman, 519–33. Englewoods Cliffs, NJ: Prentice-Hall, 1973.
Smith, Huston. *The World Religions*. New York: Harper Collins, 1991.
Stumpf, Samuel. *Philosophy: History and Problems*. 5th ed. New York: McGraw-Hill, 1994.
Suzuki, D. T. *An Introduction to Zen Buddhism*. New York: Grove, 1964.
Swami Prabhupada. *Bhagavad Gita as It Is*. Los Angles: Bhaktivedanta Book Trust, 1972.
Tillich, Paul. *A Complete History of Christian Thought*. New York: Harper & Row, 1968.
———. *Dynamics of Faith*. New York: Harper Torch, 1957.
———. *Shaking of the Foundations*. New York: Scribner's Sons, 1948.

SELECTED BIBLIOGRAPHY

———. *Systematic Theology*. Vol. 1. Chicago: University of Chicago Press, 1951.
The Upanishads. Translated and edited by Swami Nikhilananda. New York: Torchbooks, 1964.
Van Voorst. *Anthology of World Scriptures*. 3rd ed. Belmont, CA: Wadsworth, 2000.
Weisz, Paul. *The Science of Zoology*. New York: McGraw-Hill, 1966.
Whitehead, Alfred North. *Religion in the Making*. New York: New American Library, 1954.
Wilson, Edward. *The Social Conquest of Earth*. New York: Liveright, 2012.
Yogananda, Paramahansa. *Sayings of Paramahansa Yogananda*. Los Angeles: Self-Realization Fellowship, 1986.
Yogi Ramacharaka. *The Philosophies and Religions of India*. Chicago: Yogi, 1930.

www.ingramcontent.com/pod-product-compliance
Lightning Source LLC
Chambersburg PA
CBHW020856160426

43192CB00007B/945